EDUCATION AND DEVELOPMENT IN THE THIRD WORLD

Education and Development in the Third World

RICHARD D'AETH
Professor of Education
Exeter University

SAXON HOUSE|LEXINGTON BOOKS

Published by
SAXON HOUSE, D. C. Heath Ltd
Westmead, Farnborough, Hants., England

Jointly with
LEXINGTON BOOKS, D. C. Heath & Co.
Lexington, Mass., USA

ISBN 0 347 01083 0

Library of Congress Catalog Card Number 75-28616

Printed in Great Britain by
Robert MacLehose & Co. Ltd
Printers to the University of Glasgow

Contents

1 Education in Developing Countries: the Need for Re-appraisal

The heart of the problem

Education is inherently a controversial field of theory and practical action, for it is concerned both with fundamental human rights and the nurturing of personality and also with social change and the ideals at which it should aim. Thus it is personal, social and political. In the modern highly industrialised nations, commonly referred to as the 'advanced' nations, education is a massive institutional development. It usually takes a larger share of the national budget than anything else, and constitutes a full time occupation for all the young from the age of about five to fifteen or twenty or more. Moreover, the notion is growing that voluntary continuing education should be a feature of the full human life span. Many aspects of this huge development in modern society are keenly criticised, but there is little sign that it will be fundamentally changed: it appears to be a central feature of urban life in the fast changing modern technological age. The criticisms of de-schoolers and others will produce marginal changes: and perhaps future technology will replace teachers more extensively, but this prospect has made little headway as yet. Many are not happy about the effects of modern technological development on human life and happiness; but few envisage that progress on these lines can be reversed to bring back a pre-industrial age, though everyone hopes it can be controlled to prevent the further erosion of the human environment.

The situation in 'developing' countries is in marked contrast. They are by definition the nations that have not developed industrial urbanised societies with their massive educational institutions, though they often appear to be developing the latter more rapidly than their economic growth requires or can support. The criticisms of education are widespread, forceful and penetrating. The main criticism has been that the 'Western' type of schooling – which applies to the full scale extended schooling of USA, Russia, Japan and other industrialised nations as well as to Western Europe – is quite unsuited to predominantly agricultural societies.[1] Its bookish nature separates young people from the land, and does not grow out of their own culture. It was an external form of schooling imposed on colonies to meet the limited needs of their circumstances, or developed in other countries which, though politically independent, were under foreign economic domination. Among the consequences were disruption of indigenous societies, without the encouragement of new social relationships and loyalties. These and similar criticisms have been so far-reaching that the need for new policies in many countries cannot be ignored. Moreover, most developing countries cannot afford a full scale system of education, even if it were desirable; so that it has become necessary either to restrict formal schooling to a minority, or develop alternative kinds of education. That choice has to be faced. But each developing country has its own characteristics and educational problems – even those in the group with the lowest income per head of population differ widely from one another. It is an important theme of this book that the failure to give sufficient weight to the full range of circumstances affecting educational development in each country, and the tendency to see an over simplified relationship between the expansion of education and economic growth, have led to the present sense of disillusionment.

Education and development: recent changes in outlook

The notion that 'education' – which is commonly assumed to include schooling for all children, as well as adult literacy – is an integral part of 'development' is fairly recent, still imperfectly understood, and now undergoing critical analysis and reassessment. Although we are still in the middle of these changes it may be appropriate to look briefly at them in perspective.

Until the First World War it was largely taken for granted that the Great Powers would continue to govern their colonies or exercise economic domination over less developed nations. A natural consequence was that when the League of Nations was established after the end of the war to form the first international organisation of governments, it was on this basis; thus it seemed appropriate to take away Germany's colonies and, instead of proposing early independence, place them in a form of trusteeship. For it was then assumed that colonies might grow to political maturity and independence through a slow process taking a number of generations.

The second phase came after the Second World War, when the more widely based United Nations replaced the League of Nations, and it provided a world forum of opinion in favour of ending colonialism. However, it was not until most colonies gained their independence in the 1960s that the 'poor' nations became numerous in the Assembly of the United Nations – where they are now a majority – and began to press their claims, though at first with little effect, for the economic divide between rich nations and poor was shown to be growing wider and not narrower.

The third phase occurred with dramatic suddenness in late 1973, when the oil producing nations quadrupled the price of oil, and in so doing precipitated a more or less revolutionary upheaval in the world economic order. Almost overnight these nations, which were among the least 'developed', jumped into the front rank of international financial influence; and when their voice was joined with the other 'less developed' countries which lacked oil riches, it was backed for the first time with economic power. This has already caused a transformation of the world scene, not only in economic relationships, but also in world problems of aid, resources, population, food, pollution etc. – quite apart from the crucial underlying problems of reducing international tensions and preserving world peace.

This brief summary indicates three phases by which the 'less developed' nations have come to the front of the international economic and political scene. Underlying the transition from one phase to the next, however, are profound changes in attitude and understanding, both involving long, slow processes very different from the recent sudden economic metamorphosis. Yet the forming of new attitudes provides the motivation for political pressures and hence the driving force for change. However, a deeper understanding of economic relationships – the balance between prices of raw materials, food and manufactured goods; the problems of international banking; the influence of multinational companies, and so on – and of all the complex social and cultural aspects of 'development', are also required to provide a rational basis for national policies.

Educational problems have to be considered in a broad context. Practical questions about the syllabuses of primary or secondary schools, how to teach literacy, or how to train mechanics are important; but they are closely related to more general issues, such as how the system of formal education should be related to the traditional culture, including its religious and spiritual values and the social relationships of family and society, and how these can be related in turn to the development of a modern democracy. To improve the standard of living in a poor country – or of poor persons in a rich country – is a necessary first step. But now it is accepted everywhere that this material criterion is by itself a far too limited aim for 'development', which has to be expressed in terms of the 'quality of living'; and this involves human qualities and the culture and traditions of each country, and often of different societies within a country.[2] There can be no single blueprint; for the aims should correspond with the marvellously rich variety of cultures in the world, with enough flexibility to allow the lively expression of individual personality.

However, our outlook on the aims of development is bound to be tempered by the circumstances of the time. When changes are as rapid and unpredictable as in the recent economic upheaval, it is hard to visualise the consequences with clarity. Ideas about what the aims should be, especially in the short term, are bound to be affected; and this emerges clearly in the field of education.

The 'winds of change' and the ending of colonialism

The end of the Second World War brought the final twilight of empires after many centuries during which successive empires had grown, blossomed and faded. One major part of the British Empire, the great subcontinent of India, which had been moving towards independence before the war, was almost granted it as a single nation, and then finally divided tragically on religious lines in 1947 to form India and Pakistan, the latter comprising two widely separated parts. It was a difficult birth, and the early years were turbulent, leading finally to a civil war which severed the two parts of Pakistan, leaving both grievously weakened. India itself has continued as a united country, an outstanding achievement, despite great economic difficulties and a tremendous increase in population, though with democracy seeming to falter in 1975. India, however, with her rich and ancient cultures, political maturity and close approach to independence before the war, was a special case. The Philippines were in a comparable situation, and gained their political independence from the USA at the same time. Other colonies were much less advanced, and the main wave of independence did not come until nearly fifteen years later.

Moreover, when the fighting and destruction of the Second World War were over, the nations of Europe were exhausted, struggling to rebuild their shattered economies and former conditions of living, and no longer the confident leaders of empires. The war had been accompanied by much talk of freedom and equality, and of rebuilding a better world; and the technology of war accelerated the development of mass communication, in television as well as radio, which spread infectious ideas about liberty and international news widely round the world – except in the communist bloc where freedom of information and discussion is strictly limited. The subsequent development of portable transistor radios made it technically possible for mass communication to reach isolated rural communities and this remarkable transformation took place within a decade. The only limitations to the spread of information and ideas are now political.

In many colonies political organisations were formed and began to press

4

for independence. Under these conditions, when Macmillan as Prime Minister of Britain visited Africa and used the phrase 'winds of change' in a speech in 1960, it caught on everywhere. Colonies were, with few exceptions, by then expressing their desire for independence more vociferously, and in some cases militantly. The tacit prewar assumption that they would grow slowly to maturity over an indefinitely long period was no longer tenable. New constitutions giving more or less complete internal self-government were granted by Britain and France to most of their colonial territories in Africa, Asia and the Caribbean, and the tide of political pressure soon gathered momentum. It was accompanied by bitter fighting at times, as in Vietnam, Indonesia and Algeria, but for the most part the convulsions were peaceful in spite of the profound changes of attitude required, especially when large empires were being dissolved; and in Western Europe only Portugal stood firm against change. Once the process of gaining independence had started, it spread with increasing speed. For instance, in West Africa the three strongest colonies led the way, Ghana in 1957 and Nigeria and Senegal in 1960, while nine more followed almost at once (Sierra Leone, Mauritania, Mali, Guinea, Upper Volta, Ivory Coast, Togo, Dahomey and Niger), leaving only Gambia (1965) and finally, after a prolonged struggle, the Portuguese colonies (1975 or later). In many instances the boundaries of these new states made little sense in terms of geography, race, language, religion or history; for they were artificial units formed out of the haphazard rivalries of the colonial powers. Moreover, the changes had often come with un-expected suddenness, and there had been little preparation for independence. Two extreme examples of this are given by Zaire, formerly the Belgian Congo, which had fewer than thirty university graduates when it was hurriedly granted independence, to administer a population of some twenty million in an area four times that of Belgium and France combined; and Libya, with a population of nearly two million, which did not have a secondary school for its own people until four years before independence was granted in 1961. In other countries the situation was much more favourable, but nearly all had formidable tasks in creating a political system that would attempt to combine wide representation, freedom of expression and strong leadership; for these were envisaged as being in varying degrees essential to foster a sense of national unity, and to develop a modern economy in the struggle against widespread poverty. The difficulties have certainly been formidable, and still are. But it was abundantly clear that the colonies were all determined to gain their freedom to make their own political decisions whether or not they could be truly independent economically or in trained personnel. Being free did not solve their problems, and sometimes created fresh difficulties; but it did give them self-respect. It was as though it had ended a kind of slave

5

relationship between nations, as the slavery of individuals had eventually been terminated, at least officially, by most nations, in the nineteenth century.

How the name 'Third World' originated

The 'Third World' is a generic name for the very poor, mostly ex-colonial, countries of Africa, Asia and Latin America, which has become widely used in the last fifteen years. The extensive adoption of the name did not indicate a new approach to poverty, which has afflicted most of the world's population throughout the history of mankind, but a fresh perspective on the political significance of these very poor countries. They were first called *Le Tiers Monde* in France, where nonaligned countries were seen as forming a new third group, in contradistinction to the First World of the capitalist Western nations (including the USA and others of similar character) and the Second World of the communist Eastern bloc. At that time, in the late 1950s, the USSR still maintained its rigid isolation by the impenetrable 'iron curtain' from the Western world, and the resulting 'cold war' which had followed the ending of hostilities of the Second World War showed no hint of a thaw. The irreconcilable division between the capitalist and communist blocs kept fears of nuclear war close to the surface; and some of those concerned for world peace even hoped that the nonaligned nations of the Third World might be able to make a new approach in the efforts to resolve the impasse between the First and Second Worlds. Thus the notion behind the new name when it first came into use was essentially political, as a new force on the divided world scene.

However, soon afterwards, Russia began to talk with Europe and the USA, *détente* eased the tension, and in the changed circumstances the hope that the Third World might take a fresh political initiative faded quietly into the background. It would have been a forlorn hope anyway, for all that these nations then had in common was great poverty, and in other respects their situations were extremely varied. Some had been politically independent for a long time, though many of these – like the nations of South America – were far from being economically independent. Several, including India and Pakistan, had become independent at the end of the Second World War, a few more recently; and some in parts of Africa, Asia and the Caribbean, still seemed to be a long way from becoming independent. Against this background, the development of education was slow. There was a gradual expansion in some colonies as a preparation for the long-term coming of independence, though in others there was hardly any provision of secondary or higher education. Progress was also slow in the independent countries, for most of them had few natural resources to help reduce poverty, and in some of them privileged minorities were strong enough to retain power and resist social change. In brief, there could be little development of education in these poor countries while political, economic and social conditions were so unfavourable: for education is not an independent variable, but has always to be seen in a wider context.

The pressure for economic development

During the early post-colonial years the United Nations provided a world forum in which the representatives of small as well as large nations could join in discussion of world problems. Though it has been generally ineffective in taking action to enforce its resolutions, its specialised agencies – UNESCO, FAO, WHO, ILO etc. – have done valuable service in collecting and disseminating reputable information covering all member nations, as well as in undertaking a wide range of development studies and projects. As representatives of the newly independent nations swelled the ranks of the General Assembly, the realisation became abundantly clear that two-thirds of the population of the world lived in abject poverty and on the borderline of starvation; that this was the overriding problem of the mixed group of poor nations of the Third World; and that this situation could only be ignored by the advanced countries at their peril.

The first task was to give economic aid to raise the extremely low standards of living and reduce the risk of widespread famine, on grounds of humanity. However, the newly independent countries pressed their aspirations harder, bent on reducing the gap between the rich nations and the poor by achieving rapid economic growth, and at the same time developing a universal system of modern education, health etc. The response of the advanced nations has been considerable and on a rising scale. Some individual countries, not always those with most resources, have developed notable aid programmes; and UNESCO and other international agencies have been giving substantial assistance. But the contributions have been a very small fraction of the resources of the advanced countries, the aid has generally been on their conditions and the terms of international trade have been in their favour, with the result that the benefits for the poor countries have been largely counterbalanced. There is no doubt that this has happened, though where the balance of advantage lies is controversial and naturally varies from one situation to another.[3] The motives for giving aid have been complex – humanitarian, pressure in a competitive world for trade advantages and to secure raw materials, political alliances, anxiety to avoid international stresses that might lead to another large scale war – and it is little wonder that aid has not always flowed to the most deserving countries or the most efficiently planned projects. Nevertheless it can fairly be said that the main stress has been on aid for economic growth in the nations of the Third World, in an effort to satisfy their urgent desire to 'catch up' as quickly as possible, during the first UN development decade from 1960 to 1970, and again in the current decade, now half way through.

How successful have these efforts, concentrated on the economic front, been? It is clear that over the last decade or two, for which adequate statistics are available, economic aid has failed to narrow the yawning gap between the advanced industrial nations and most of the predominantly agricultural countries of the Third World, for its advantages have been more than offset by adverse terms of trade and conditions of aid. The gap between rich and poor has been growing wider. Improving agriculture lowers the danger of starvation, but appears to contribute little to national prosperity, while industrial development has been a handicap race hopelessly loaded against the late starters, with the rich firmly in control of international trade. The economic situation cannot, however, be considered in isolation. With populations rising fast in the poor countries, and world reserves of food diminishing to a dangerously low level, the risk of famine seems to be drawing closer for hundreds of millions of people. Another consequence of the rapidly increasing population has been that the number of illiterates in the world is rising inexorably, in spite of large scale literacy campaigns and massive expenditure on expanding school systems. The outcome of the vigorous aid programmes, and all the efforts of international agencies, seem to have achieved little more than relieving the symptoms, easing the pressures of frustration and conflict between the 'haves' and the 'have nots', without getting near to resolving the fundamental problems. Inevitably there is some disillusionment and much questioning among all those concerned with aid programmes, not on the importance of the venture or on the need to sustain and enlarge programmes of aid, but on analysing what are the basic problems and how to resolve them; and among the receiving nations of the Third World much talk of 'neocolonialism' and a growing feeling that the balance of international economics is tilted hopelessly against them and must be changed by raising the relative price of other raw materials in the wake of oil.

Education in the 1960s: high hopes and growing doubts

Most countries that gained their political independence within the last decade or two placed much of their faith for improving living conditions on

8

the expansion of education, and gave a major share of their budgets to it; far more so than in the advanced countries, where it is largely taken for granted, even though it now absorbs more of the national budget than either 'defence' or health and other social services. In the advanced countries the educational system is a massive bureaucratic organisation, whose main growth is now at the tertiary level, employing so many teachers and administrators that its inertia makes it very resistant to change, even to a considerable extent insulated from national political or economic pressures. In the Third World, however, the relationship of education to politics and the national economy is far more direct, for it is viewed essentially as a vital contributor to economic growth and to the expression of political ideas about the form society should take, whether traditional and élitist or progressively socialist, either resisting the materialism of the advanced industrial nations or incorporating much of their culture. Hence the problems of educational development have to be considered in an economic and political context.

The political leaders of Third World nations have been under great pressure to provide free primary or elementary schooling for all children. Education is one of the basic rights set out by the United Nations, the overcoming of ignorance was a means to improving the quality of life, and an adequate supply of trained people is needed at all levels to run a modern state independently and to achieve rapid economic growth. There were many formulations in government plans for the development of education, usually couched in idealistic rather than practical terms, and often expressing hopes such as the following:

1   That better education would overcome ignorance and so open the way for individuals to lead richer lives, to establish better social relationships within communities, and so enable the local communities to gain in self-respect and become more democratic and responsible, more able to take initiatives for their own improvement and to become more outward looking.

2   That to improve education would contribute to economic growth, thus raising the general standard of living, and helping towards better employment opportunities, health, housing etc.

3   That education would improve the quality of rural life, especially the level of agricultural skills with the aid of literacy, and the opportunities for a richer cultural life.

4   That it would improve the training in skills for the development of industries, and also modern social services, increasing the readiness to learn new techniques required for innovation and change.

5   That it would be the most effective means of developing a more equitable

9

society, with better opportunities for individuals in the countryside as well as in towns, with less extremes of poverty and affluence, more responsible leaders and administrators. Hopefully such a society would have fewer tensions and frustrations, and so be more satisfied and peaceful.

6 That education would contribute to nation building, by fostering a growing respect for each nation's own culture and traditions, and by aiding the development of political maturity, which would be capable of combining orderly leadership with freedom of thought and expression, and respect for individual rights.

Such were the hopes of the new political leaders, expressed in a variety of ways, and often set out as a preamble to ambitious plans for the expansion of their educational system. Such statements reflect the idealism of the first post-independence phase, before financial limitations had begun to bite, and before there had been time to think critically about some of the underlying educational problems.

There was evidence of some preparatory thinking on these lines years before, in a limited way, as in the plan set out well before independence by the government of the Western Region of Nigeria:

> The principles that must be given due consideration in any educational policy today are economic, political and cultural . . . The economic principle that must underlie educational policy is one which aims at a comprehensive economic development of the country . . . Any political principle governing educational policy at the present stage of our development must regard as a top priority the provision of such an education as will establish the most vigorous form of self-government and independence. . . . We want men in whom the elements of European civilization are fully integrated and harmonized with indigenous African culture, men without mental dichotomy.

The great surge at independence was in the first place to provide schooling for all children, even if it meant only four years of schooling in cheap buildings with ill paid teachers, often with curricula and textbooks based on those of former colonial powers or other advanced countries. The three major regional conferences organised by UNESCO in Addis Ababa, Karachi and Santiago de Chile in the early 1960s demonstrated the enormous numbers of additional teachers and school buildings needed for expansion on these lines; and this was fully borne out by the subsequent regional and national development plans for education. Before long the cost of these expansion programmes far exceeded what most governments could afford, and it became necessary to decide what should be given priority. In Africa especially, where the shortage of trained persons was acute, in contrast to India and South America, it seemed more important to develop secondary education than to aim at providing primary or elementary schools for all children. At the same time, advanced education, technical as well as at university level, was seen as an essential development.

Wherever there was a serious lack of trained persons, the techniques of 'manpower planning' provided a natural approach. In this field the Report of the Ashby Committee, which was presented to the Nigerian government on the eve of independence in 1960, was seminal.[4] It showed the value of manpower planning, and how the systems of higher education could be developed to meet the requirements of trained personnel for economic growth and for national self-reliance. It proposed that this development should be accelerated by the short term importing of teachers and other trained experts in key positions for expansion. The report broke new ground in several ways: the committee itself represented a partnership, having three British, three American and three Nigerian members; its timing coincided neatly with political independence; and it made imaginative proposals for giving aid to accelerate the development of higher education so that Nigeria could be enabled to meet its own requirements at an early date (i.e. within 20 years). Not surprisingly, it had a far-reaching influence on the planning of education in other countries; but, as might be expected of a competent exercise in quantative planning, it did not examine the underlying educational questions, tacitly assuming that schools, colleges and universities would continue to develop more or less on existing lines.

The educational dilemma

The nations of the Third World began to see their dilemma more clearly. Their aim should be to strive for highly developed systems of education like those of the advanced countries, because that is how Western Europe, North America, Russia and Japan were seen to have succeeded; but they could not afford it. What they envisaged as 'development', in the sense of a Western type of economy and educational system, was turning out to be a mirage – always receding out of reach.

The realisation that the early aspirations to provide schools for all children were far beyond the reach of the Third World became increasingly clear as governments struggled with budgets, and as UNESCO published surveys and statistics; and the gulf between hopes and reality were portrayed convincingly in 1969 by Coombs in his book *The World Educational Crisis*.[5] The cost of universal primary and secondary education would be far beyond the resources of poor countries. The UNESCO regional plans, e.g. that for South East Asia, had shown how overwhelming was the task of attempting to copy the educational systems of advanced countries: an undeveloped economy could not support an advanced system of education, even if it were appropriate. The failure was, however, just as much in the quality of education as in the quantity.

The aim of having fully developed Western-type systems of schooling was coming under double fire: not only was it too expensive, but also there was growing criticism of the bookish schooling as being quite unsuited to predominantly agricultural societies, ignoring their language, literature, religion, traditions and customs, in the broadest sense their culture. This was the schooling developed in colonial times or under the influence of a dominating advanced country, infused with a foreign culture, intended to educate a minority to help run the country, and in all these respects divorced from modern needs. Not infrequently it contributed to social breakdown, within families and communities, spreading restlessness and a lack of sense of belonging among the young. It produced too few skilled workers, and yet in many countries at the same time produced too many secondary school leavers, giving rise to severe unemployment. Too often education was dissociated from the needs of society. So the criticisms ran, though it would be unfair for education to bear all the blame. For instance, unsuitable schooling is often described as a cause of the migration of rural youth to cities, or rather to unemployment in shanty towns, but the causes of this widespread phenomenon are certainly more complex (see chapter 6). The irrelevance of book learning to rural communities in which the great majority of Third World children grow up and live has been fiercely criticised; so have the futility of meaningless rote learning in school, the rigidity of a school curriculum fettered by examinations, the dominance of the humanities in a liberal education at the expense of agriculture and technology, the production through the academic selection process of a new priviliged élite; the list merely serves to show the gravity of the problem.

A note of caution is already overdue about the danger of generalisations. The countries of the Third World have in common a very low per capita income, and certain features like wretchedly poor diet, health, housing, education and so on, that are concomitants of a low income; but they are also very varied in their characteristics, and in the related educational problems. For instance, the former colonial territories of sub-Sahara Africa had a serious shortage of educated persons at all levels, including graduates. The extreme situation in Zaire has already been mentioned; and countries like Ghana, Senegal, Nigeria and Uganda, in spite of having their own universities, still had serious shortages. In contrast, the countries of South America

12

in which there is such widespread poverty that the average per capita income is low, nevertheless have a large, well educated and prosperous middle class; the weakness in many of these countries is not shortage of trained persons, but in the political, social and economic structure which is resistant to democratic development. A different situation again occurs in some countries of Asia, from India to the Philippines, where there is a chronic surplus of graduates far beyond the absorptive capacity of the economy, which is shackled by heavy and increasing overpopulation in relation to resources. These examples stretch from one extreme to the other, from a serious shortage of highly educated persons to a large surplus of them; yet all are poor countries of the Third World. And if we examine other characteristics, such as political, social and cultural features, equally significant divergences will emerge.

In spite of all the variations between one country and another, however, the powerful magnetism of Western influences cannot be ignored (it need hardly be said that these influences now come at least as much from North America as from Western Europe). The provision of full secondary education for all children on increasingly comprehensive lines, and of extensive and varied higher education with full supporting grants for students – these are features of advanced systems of education to which all countries (or nearly all, as we shall see later) would like to aspire if their conditions allowed. Yet the advanced countries are criticising their own systems more and more: the poor and disadvantaged are not being sufficiently helped, schools do not overcome handicaps of family or race, the educational system is not proving to be by itself a social leveller or a means of reforming society. Also, while governments continue the trend of extending the duration of schooling, the young express a different view. Many of them wish to gain their independence earlier, leaving school when they are ready; to be more free in choosing what advanced studies to follow, and when, avoiding the climb up a single career ladder; to be more concerned about social reform, more international in outlook. Insofar as there is truth in these comments, several awkward questions are posed. Are some developing countries aspiring to copy features of education in advanced countries which are already dissolving away or undergoing fundamental changes? Should more attention be paid to community colleges, open universities, recurrent education: how should these and other alternatives be evaluated? Perhaps even nearer to the heart of the problem, for well over half the population of the world live in rural areas: should schools play a smaller part, and a variety of non-formal activities a larger one, in the pattern of educational development? There are certainly no clear cut 'models' to follow, and it is necessary to analyse the situation in each developing country, starting with objectives; for, however difficult these are to define, they provide the only basis for rational assessment.

Notes

[1] Rene Dumont, *False Start in Africa* (translated from French: *L'Afrique noir est mal partie*), Andre Deutsch, London, 1966/2nd. ed. 1969.
R. Apthorpe (ed.), *People Planning and Development Studies*, Frank Cass, London, 1970.
[2] A. Curle, *Educational Strategy for Developing Societies*, Tavistock, London, 1963/2nd ed. 1970.
G. Hunter, *Best of Both Worlds? A Challenge on Development Policies in Africa*, Oxford University Press, London, 1967.
[3] Tibor Mende, *From Aid to Re-Colonization: Lessons of a Failure*, Harrap, London, 1974.
D. Wall, *The Charity of Nations: The Political Economy of Foreign Aid*, Macmillan, London, 1973.
[4] *Investment in Education* (Report of Ashby Commission), Federal Ministry of Education, Lagos, 1960.
[5] P. H. Coombs, *The World Educational Crisis – A Systems Analysis*, Oxford University Press, New York, 1968.
G. Z. F. Bereday, *Essays on World Education: The Crisis of Supply and Demand*, Oxford University Press, New York, 1969.

2 Education in Developing Countries and the World Scene of the 1970s

Recent events affecting education

We have seen how the idealism of the newly independent nations of the Third World led them to place high hopes during the 1960s on the expansion of education as a means of narrowing the gulf separating them from the advanced countries, and how this idealism was gradually replaced by realism: a poor country could not afford the educational system of an advanced industrial country – but was that what would really suit its needs? Was it reasonable in the light of the experience of the advanced countries to expect education to lead the way in transforming society? Once it was accepted that education should not be expected to play a leading role on its own, but should be part of an overall national strategy for development, the process of re-appraisal could begin; and this opened the way for serious thought to be given to fundamental reforms. It seems likely that this process of re-appraisal and reform will lead during the later 1970s to the transformation of education in the Third World, and that it will be profoundly affected by four very different, though not unrelated, major changes on the international scene:

1 The emergence of China from its seclusion.
2 The dramatic rise in the price of oil, which has produced a shock change in the world economic balance.
3 The growing political importance of the Third World.
4 The increasing realisation that problems of population, food, raw materials, pollution etc., call for treatment on a world basis, hence the notion of 'one world'.

The potential influence of China

The opening chapter recounted how the name Third World, and the concept which it involved, originated in the 'cold war' between USSR on the one hand and Europe and the USA on the other, during the years which followed the Second World War. The changeover from this militant confrontation to a period of negotiation, even though only on a very limited basis, transformed the world political scene. An event of no less profound importance took place in 1973 when mainland China, having consolidated its revolution which had transformed the lives of a fifth of the world's population, opened its windows to look cautiously on the outside world, and its doors to let a few acceptable foreigners in; allowing at the same time a modest expansion of international trade, and becoming a member of the United Nations. Its appeal to the Third World has naturally been tremendous, for it is a predominantly rural country with natural resources that are adequate but hardly very rich in relation to the size of its population; and it has carried through a social revolution, abolishing the former privileged classes, and developing the vast countryside, with only limited industrialisation. Moreover, all this has been achieved without foreign investment or skills (after the Russians were asked to leave).

At first sight it seems to have achieved what others have only dreamed about – though few countries have such strong traditions of social discipline that they would readily accept the long hours of unremitting work, and the regimentation of behaviour and thought. The nature of the new society is deeply rooted in the Chinese character, and in the ancient culture which pervades all aspects of their individual lives to an extent that reflects the continuity of many centuries; while the new political unity was forged in the desperate struggle for survival in the war with Japan, when much of their country was devastated. Certainly no country outside the Chinese culture – Vietnam and much of Korea, for example, have in the past been confluent with it – could think of copying the achievements of the Maoist revolution; of which we can as yet have only a tentative appreciation, and which may still go through further upheavals of doctrine and practice before it reaches a more mature stability. But China will certainly have an enormous attraction for many developing countries, because it seems to have achieved a revolution based mainly on an agrarian economy, giving a far more equal and coopera- tive form of society, with true independence from the great industrial powers of East or West, and with an idealism that has forged a national unity of tremendous power. This could become a major influence on the Third World during the next decade.

Most countries of the Third World have pursued policies aiming at more democratisation, preserving individual liberty while reducing poverty and increasing equality in society. In their different circumstances this is true of countries in all parts of the world e.g. India, Sri Lanka, Malaysia and else- where in Asia, many parts of Africa and South America; though often the political will or the economic framework are too weak to allow much change,

and in nearly all cases the high rate of population increase which is characteristic of poor countries offsets the drive for progress. In a few, however, a
more revolutionary approach has been attempted, as in Cuba, Chile or
Tanzania. Cuba has been caught between the cross fire of USSR and USA,
which makes it hard to assess its progress in social reform, though it seems
that the early zeal has settled to a more levelheaded effort for development.
In Chile the effort to carry through democratically a revolution to a far more
equal form of socialist society was overturned by American influence exerted
through the government's Central Intelligence Agency. Tanzania is attempting, under the outstanding leadership of President Nyerere, to establish its
own modern socialist form of society, while preserving as far as possible its
political and economic independence. The stresses while it seeks to build,
with few resources, its indigenous form of socialism, may cause unmanage-
able difficulties; but the efforts will be watched with much goodwill and
anxiety, for they could have far-reaching significance.

Oil and the new economic balance

The second recent change has been the sudden large increase in the price of
oil successfully enforced by the main oil producing countries of the Middle
East in late 1973, first as a political sanction against the nations supporting
Israel in the recurrent Arab–Israeli war, and then carried on with the aim of
altering dramatically the economic balance between the advanced industrial
nations for whom oil is the life blood of energy, and the relatively undeveloped nations rich in oil resources. The war-induced unity of the main
oil producing nations has shown how strong their position is, and how
vulnerable many of the industrial nations are in their economies. This
dramatic confrontation led to a fourfold increase in the price of oil within a
few months from the end of 1973. It has dislocated the delicate framework of
international finance, and produced a new balance of economic power.
From quite a different angle it reinforces the doubts about industrial
economies based on ever increasing consumption, and on vast production of
armaments both for 'defence' and for external trade – and so again leads to
questioning about motives and ideals, especially about the form societies
should take. It is too early yet to distinguish what the consequences of this
profound change in world economic power will be, even assuming that
renewed Arab–Israeli fighting, and the risk it would bring of a conflagration
involving major powers, can be avoided. But it is bound to divide the
former countries of the Third World into two polarised groups – the oil
producers, which have suddenly acquired such huge wealth that they plan to

develop advanced industrial economies almost from scratch in one generation; and the others, whose difficulties are magnified by the steep increases in the cost of imported oil, and in turn of fertilisers, industrial equipment, even food, on which their own development hinges. Thus, the oil producers will attempt to jump out of the Third World into the First in one generation with all the violent economic and social stresses this is likely to involve; while most of the nations of the Third World will have to face even greater difficulties and the strains of slower development. The early indications are that the oil producers of the Middle East will be inclined to invest their new fortunes mainly in the advanced countries in order to give stronger support to their own economic development, while providing aid for selected Third World countries with which they have close political and religious associations; although it is significant that the Kuwait Fund for Arab Economic Development, which was established in 1964, now makes some loans to non-Arab countries and cooperates with the World Bank on certain projects, and other Arab countries are beginning to follow suit.

The Third World exerts political pressure

The struggle to end colonialism has been almost completely won, but the problems of overcoming extreme poverty remain as intractable as ever, with the gap between the poor nations and the rich industrial ones becoming wider. In most former colonial countries a new indigenous élite has taken over from the former colonial élite, and holds on to the same privileges. In much of the Third World military régimes have replaced elected politicians, with a natural tendency to be strongly conservative, although some are liberal, like the military government of Nigeria at present; and a few are controlled by extreme left-wing groups, as appears to be the case in Ethiopia. In most countries the advantages of economic development go largely to the middle classes which form a small minority, and the mass of the population continues to exist at bare subsistence level in the countryside, constantly threatened by droughts and other natural disasters, or in the squalid congestion of the urban shanty towns. The great hopes of even a decade ago have been dimmed. It is not that the many fine aid projects have not been worthwhile, but simply that even when planned and executed in admirable co-operation between donor and recipient (which has by no means always happened), their impact has been on far too small a scale to offset the massive advantages of the industrial nations. Without these aid projects the situation would almost certainly be worse still, and more hopeless; but the Third World is beginning to feel its strength, is not interested in simply having more aid, and wishes to establish new relationships with the advanced nations based to a much greater extent on mutual respect, with a more equal sharing of resources, and a fairer relationship between the price of their primary exports and the industrial products they import.

The change of mood among the nations of the Third World since the 'oil crisis' was clearly revealed in a series of important UN conferences which took place during 1974 on raw materials, world population and food supplies (there was also a conference on the exploitation of the sea, which is less directly relevant here). Some of the implications of these conferences, in so far as they form a background for educational development, are considered in the following sections.

Raw materials and development

The first of these conferences was a special session of the UN Assembly called by the chairman of the nonaligned nations, which includes all the developing countries – who call themselves the Group of 77, thus having a majority in the General Assembly of 138 nations when they vote together – to consider the problems of raw materials in relation to development. Frustrated by trying for many years without success in the United Nations Conference on Trade and Development (UNCTAD) and other forums to persuade the rich countries to increase aid and improve the terms of trade, these nations pressed their case resolutely. Aid had declined from 0·53 per cent per annum of Gross National Product in 1961 to 0·35 per cent in 1971, only half the target agreed by the UN donor nations at the beginning of the second development decade; and the rich countries had continued to control both the price of their exports and the world market for their imports. Only when the developing countries control their own resources and regulate the prices of their exports, or at least enter the process of bargaining on a more or less equal basis, can they have a chance of rising out of their poverty. Their need is great, for with 70 per cent of the world's population they have only 30 per cent of its resources; over three hundred million children are suffering from malnutrition, and starvation is widespread; a fifth of adult males are more or less unemployed, and the population is increasing faster than employment. Their proposals at the special session included the right to nationalise their natural resources and control the prices for them; the encouragement of indigenous industries; more and better aid; special help for the poorest countries; and a new international economic order. It was significant that the newly rich Arab oil countries, and others with oil such as Nigeria, Venezuela, Algeria and Indonesia, held together with those Third World countries which have been made even poorer by the steep rise in the price of oil. The representative of Sierra Leone expressed the feeling among the developing countries:

There are certain fundamentals on the issues before us on which we are all agreed, and which need no extensive elaboration. We are agreed that the political independence which our various countries have been able to win over the years is being constantly devalued through economic exploitation. We are agreed that our interests are not taken into consideration when vital economic matters affecting the lives of our people come up for discussion on the international agenda. We are agreed that except we organize ourselves to protect our own interests in the same way as the developed countries organize themselves to protect their own interests, our situation in the Third World will get worse. We are agreed that serious exploitation of our rich natural resources continues to take place in spite of our so-called independence. We are agreed that the present extremely unequal economic relations must be changed.

Although the Third World has been divided between those nations which have suddenly become rich through oil and those which have been made even poorer (it has been suggested that the latter should be termed the Fourth World), they are united by deep resentment over years of unfair economic treatment and humiliation, even by the scarcely veiled criticisms involved in the application of 'performance criteria' to aid, and the many imputations of their inferiority occurring in films and other mass media. The need is to build up their self-respect, and erase the causes of resentment.

The mood which emerged clearly from this Sixth Special Assembly, held from 9 April to 2 May 1974, revealed the bitter sense of frustration which had grown over the years between the Third World and the Developed World. It was dominated by the feelings of nationalism, proclaiming the right of every nation to full permanent sovereignty over its own resources by nationalising them and controlling the prices; and pressing for a 'new economic order', which would transform patterns of trade, give special help to the poorest nations, and end neocolonialism. There was no dramatic breakthrough, but a new emphasis on what the Third World considered to be necessary for genuine cooperation for development; and the new mood became very evident in the Conference on Population which followed shortly afterwards, in August 1974. The pressure by the Third World for more equal treatment is being maintained in 1975, and will certainly be continued when the fourth UNCTAD meets in Nairobi in 1976; and its voice will be powerful if it acts in concert with the Organisation of Petroleum Exporting Countries (OPEC), as it began to do in 1974.

Population and development

The second of the conferences, to which reference has been made, was about the expansion of world population, and how it might be limited as part of programmes of socioeconomic development. This problem underlies all aspects of development, and has particular significance for education.

The modern debate on birth control was launched by Thomas Malthus when his *Essay on the Principle of Population* was published in 1789, and became a best seller. He saw population increasing in geometric ratio and soon outgrowing the production of food, which would only increase in arithmetic ratio. The 'natural' result was starvation and poverty, because the poor indulged in large families, and in his view they were in consequence of this to blame for their poverty. His views were contested, for example by William Godwin, who claimed that the real cause of poverty and starvation was the unjust organisation of society and the unfair distribution of wealth, and therefore social change was more important than sexual restraint. Since then the debate has been on two main lines, the first concerned with how to forecast the future expansion of national populations on the basis of existing demographic data; and the second with the consequences of population expansion and ways in which it might be controlled. The consideration of these issues has been lively, but it is only in the last decade or two that the problems of world population increase have come to be widely regarded as very urgent.

A clear picture of population increase has now been revealed by demographic research. The population of the world increased slowly until around the end of the eighteenth century. By that time improved hygiene and diet, spreading from Europe, began to cause world population to increase in a geometric manner, as a combined result of reducing infant mortality and lengthening the expectation of life without a corresponding reduction of fertility. The outcome of this has been that the world population doubled between 1900 and 1960, and is now in process of doubling again in a span of only thirty-five years, with a further more rapid increase ahead unless fertility rates can be reduced quickly and drastically. The present rate of increase has been expressed by many dramatic illustrations, for instance that it is equivalent to a new Chicago every two weeks.

When demographic information began to be collated on a world basis in the 1950s, it was evident that death rates were continuing to fall with advances in medicine, especially through the control of malaria and other infectious diseases, while birth rates were not declining, and in some countries were rising, especially in the Third World.[1] Pressure on the United Nations to formulate population policies was resisted for a variety of reasons, for instance by Roman Catholics on religious grounds, and by African nations seeing it as a move to prevent their countries from developing. Eventually a majority was reached in 1966 in favour of considering the problems involved, including the controversial suggestions that fertility limitation, or family planning, should be considered as a basic human right, and that people should be given the means to have the number of children they wanted. By 1970 the United Nations decided to designate 1974 as World Population Year, and planning began for a major World Population Conference to be held at Bucharest in August of that year. This conference was intended to consider population aspects of the overall United Nations' strategy for socioeconomic development and human welfare. It was recognised as being of central importance, and it was one of the most ambitious and delicate political conferences ever staged. The preparations were intensive and international, and after many consultations and five regional conferences a Draft World Population Plan of Action was produced. It represented a very wide consensus of opinion, supported by objective demographic data.

For the first time the Conference brought the statistics and forecasts prepared by internationally recognised demographic experts into the open as a basis for debate among all the UN nations about what should be done. Although population forecasts involve making difficult assumptions about what the future fertility and mortality rates are likely to be, the main facts cannot be disputed: the so-called 'population explosion' has arisen because, while the average expectation of life has lengthened, fertility rates have not in general declined, and they continue to be especially high in the Third World. The consequence of this is that the present world population of about 3·9 billion will rise to at least 6 billion by the year 2000 even if the fertility rate were reduced almost at once to replacement level (i.e. no increase), and to 7 billion if it is reduced gradually. The forecasts after that date are even more alarming. World population will rise to 8 billion by 2100 if the fertility rate could be reduced quickly to bare replacement, and to 16 billion by that date even if the fertility rate were halved by the middle of next century – that is at least a twofold, and perhaps a fourfold, increase on the present number. Even in the next five years 500 million will be added to the world's population. With much famine and widespread malnutrition already, and food production no longer rising, the immediate outlook is grim and the future much worse.

Global forecasts are inclined to seem remote from day to day living, and thus to be ignored by politicians with more immediate concerns. But the out-

22

look is especially serious for Third World countries. Their rate of increase is much above the world average, and so high is their proportion of young people – commonly 40 per cent under the age of 15 – that even strong action now would not stop their population from doubling in the next twenty-five years, though it would slow down the increase after that. The immediate situation is illustrated by India, where the population exceeds that of Latin America and Africa together, and is increasing by a million a month, the addition being equivalent to a nation the size of Australia each year. In much of Asia, which already has over half the world's population, and Latin America and Africa, the rate of increase is as high as in India, or even higher. The burden of providing food, schools, employment etc. on this scale is overwhelming.[2]

Under these circumstances it is not surprising that the movement for family planning has gained momentum after a slow start. The International Planned Parenthood Federation (IPPF) was founded at a meeting convened by Lady Rama Rau of India in 1952, and started with eight member countries at headquarters in London, and an annual budget of £1,500. By 1974 it had eighty-four member countries and a budget of $41 million. It operates in countries which together have 85 per cent of the world's population, though only a tiny fraction of the people are reached, and its programmes have been ineffective except where standards of living have been raised. There are many difficulties which have been only marginally overcome, and it has little effect in most situations as an isolated programme, yet is of crucial importance in overall development planning. It has spread to Egypt, India and many Asian countries.[2] Laws on abortion have been slowly liberalised, despite strong opposition; and a rise in the age of marriage has in some countries also helped to lower fertility rates. The tide in favour of family planning, which poor women seem to desire much more keenly than their governments, is rising, but unevenly. The Draft Plan stated that its aim was 'to help coordinate population trends and the trends of economic and social development', and stressed that an effective solution of population problems depends above all on socioeconomic transformation. Improved literacy and education tend to lead to a reduction in birth rates; but they seem to have a less important influence than raising the standard of living.

Against this background, however, the outcome of the conference at Bucharest came as a surprise and a disappointment. Important sections of the Draft Plan of Action, prepared with such careful consultation, were rejected by the politicians. Underlying their statements there was what could be described as an almost myopic nationalism, and a neurotic feeling that the advanced countries are much more concerned with reducing birth rates in the Third World than with development. Some inconvenient demographic facts

23

were firmly suppressed. The Draft Plan was attacked from many sides, with Argentine taking the lead and refusing to accept the approach that population should be treated in a peculiar and singular manner, outside the context of development, social justice and the equal distribution of wealth (for its official policy is to double its population of twenty-five million by 2000). A clause which aimed 'to give all who so desire' the information and means to practise family planning by 1985 was deleted with the support of the Vatican. Many countries with small populations and large areas of land, or in the shadow of strong neighbours, were concerned to increase their birth rates. Romania, for example, although it has improved the status of women and the level of education, encourages women to work, and attained a low birth rate, nevertheless opposed family planning and has repealed its liberal divorce laws. Some other nations, notably India, believed that their hopes of progress are being destroyed by rapid population increase, and were strongly in favour of moves to reduce fertility. Perhaps surprisingly, China saw the plan as an intrigue of the super powers, and insisted that each country should formulate its own population policy. This attack by China on what it described as the myth of the population explosion seemed inconsistent in that China appears to have an effective programme to control its own population. Strong traditions, such as early marriage and desire for large families had to be overcome, and this has been done by relating birth control to a comprehensive policy to influence individual behaviour. It has included giving support to the ideal of a family of only two children; ensuring the provision of adequate food, health care and education; achieving the emancipation of women; teaching the principles of family planning in schools, and making sure that birth control can be practised in every community with the help of the ubiquitous 'barefoot doctors'. This is a notable example of population control as part of an overall policy for development.

Much of the Draft, however, survived in the plan that was finally adopted by all states at the conference, except the Vatican. The complexity of the issues can be illustrated by mentioning very briefly the principles set out in Chapter II:

(a) the principal aim of development is to improve levels of living and the quality of life; (b) true development cannot take place in the absence of national independence; it also requires international cooperation, recognition of individual dignity, elimination of the consequences of natural disasters and elimination of discrimination in all its forms; (c) population and development are interrelated; (d) population policies are constituent elements of socio-economic objectives; (e) independent of these objectives, respect for human life is basic to all societies; (f) all couples and individuals have the right to decide freely and responsibly the number and spacing of their children and to have the education, information and means to do so; (g) the family is the basic unit of society and should be protected by legislation and policy; (h) women have the right to complete integration in development, particularly by equal participation in educational, social and political life; (i) recommendations in the Plan recognize the diversity of conditions within and among countries; (j) in forming population policies, consideration must be given to national resources, the environment and all aspects of food supply; attention must be directed to the just distribution of resources and minimization of wastage; (k) it is increasingly important that international measures should be adopted to deal with development and population problems, but they will not succeed unless the under-privileged can improve their living conditions; (l) the Plan must be sufficiently flexible to take account of changing circumstances; (m) the objectives of the Plan should be consistent with the U.N. Charter, the Declaration of Human Rights and the objectives of the Second U.N. Development Decade (it is evident that the last named, now half way through, will in any case have to be drastically revised).

These were the principles which were embodied in the plan, after vigorous discussions, against a background of demographic data and trends, and leading up to proposals for action; although what happens in the long run will depend on the extent to which consenting governments actually do what they agreed to do.

Our concern here is not primarily with problems of population control as such, even though these are certainly among the most important world problems at the present time, but with their relationship to education, and especially to education as a part of development policy. Several aspects can be singled out for comment:

1 A sharp reduction in the increase of population is a critical requirement for the world as a whole, and also for many individual nations (of which India is a good example, being on the brink of famine now, with its development programme offset by its rise in population, which will exceed 1000 million soon after the turn of the century).

2 The most hopeful approach to population control is through 'family planning' as part of an overall development programme. (China strenuously avoids emphasis on birth control and family planning, as we have seen, yet has a comprehensive approach through every channel to the idea of a two child family as normal. This approach, which has involved a fundamental change in the status of women, appears to have been unusually successful.)

3   Family planning seems in general to have been successful only in literate, equitable societies with reasonable and improving standards of living (e.g. it has succeeded in Mauritius, and failed in India in spite of intensive campaigns: a recent survey showed that, out of every hundred childbearing couples, ninety knew of it and sixty possessed detailed practical knowledge, but only twelve used it). People who cannot provide for their old age, or rely on the state, depend on having enough children surviving to maturity to support them. Large families are in general, with exceptions under favourable conditions, the result of a combination of ignorance, ill-health, high infant mortality and lack of security, all of which are associated with poverty.

4   The circumstances vary between countries, and within them, and it is therefore necessary to take account not only of religious and ethical aspects, but also of sensitive cultural implications in each situation.

5   Women who live in rural areas of the Third World form what has been describes as a 'silent majority' (perhaps more literally 'half'), living near subsistence level, often subservient to men and kept back from education and training, spending much of their time in the arduous jobs of fetching water and firewood, and working in the fields. Anything which would raise their level of living, such as giving village houses a supply of piped water, would increase their readiness to join in family planning.

6   The heart of the problem seems to lie in rural development, not simply because this is where the majority of people in the Third World live, but also because it would help to ensure an adequate world supply of food as well as tending to reduce the growth of world population.

7   The reduction of excessive consumption by the advanced nations must be coupled with the development of the Third World. It involves a substantial reduction of overconsumption and waste, and a reorientation of agriculture from the production of meat to cereals and milk. As one member of the conference expressed it, the rich countries in 1973 converted 385 million tons of cereals into meat, milk and eggs, which they did not urgently require, whereas most of this quantity of cereals could have been used to feed the starving – indirectly it was as if the rich had eaten the food of the starving. This was a theme which came up more vigorously in the UN World Food Conference held in Rome in November 1974.

The new political force of the Third World, which had become evident at the Sixth Special Session of the UN Assembly, had dominated the outcome of the Population Conference. They were not prepared to accept a reduction in the enormous rate of population increase as a part of overall socio-economic development, but only to consider it as a subordinate contribution to the new economic order. Each nation was to decide its own population policy, free from any firm recommendations about family planning or population control, which were given only in the most general terms.

There could be no doubt by this time that the Third World had become a major political force on the world scene. One consequence of this was that an inevitable confrontation was coming into the open between national and international interest, those obsessed with national sovereignty and those whose foremost concern is with human rights. It was perhaps in this respect that the conference made its most significant advance by agreeing to the universal right of individuals to freedom of choice about having children, and the means to exercise their choice. Moreover, Brazil and Nigeria, the largest nations of South America and Africa, have stated their intention of making this possible (though there are no signs of the intention being translated into action as yet). At present only a tiny minority of women (and their husbands) have the freedom to make this decision. What matters is how quickly the consenting governments can be persuaded to do what they have promised, and make the difficult transition from words to action.

Problems of interdependence: world food supply

The subject of the third United Nations conference, to which reference has been made, was world food production, which fell sharply in 1972 for the first time for more than twenty years.[3] There had been drought for six years in the Sahel, a broad band across Africa south of the Sahara, causing widespread famine from Ethiopia to inland West Africa. Then bad weather reduced crops in USSR and Southern Asia at a time when the USA was cutting back on its overproduction. Reserve stocks of food in the world suddenly dropped from more than an eighteen months' supply to about three weeks', after the Soviet Union had bought up nearly all the reserves, largely from the USA, at a price which had risen fourfold in a year and a half to a level above the reach of the developing countries. That was the situation that faced the World Food Conference in November 1974.

An emergency reserve fund was set up to meet sudden crises. That, however, is only the fringe of the problem: some 500 million are undernourished all the time, apart from widespread famines, and there is no doubt that food production has to be increased, and overconsumption reduced. But where does the responsibility for this lie? Should the USA, which is a highly efficient producer of wheat, subsidise its farmers to ensure a large output in order to export the surplus to developing countries? Or should the developing countries, which are predominantly agricultural, increase their own output and become more self-supporting? The latter seems to be more reasonable than the former, at least in a world made up of nations which put their highest priority on being independent, and withdraw from ideas of interdependence. This, however, is obviously an oversimplification. To increase the agricultural output of the Third World requires more fertiliser which is related in cost to oil; and this raises not only questions of finance, but also of reducing overconsumption of fertiliser in the advanced countries – to give only two examples, Britain could grow more food and use less, while USA and Canada are said to use more fertiliser on their golf courses than the total amount used by the Third World.

There is already an overriding need for interdependence if massive starvation is to be avoided, for the total food potential of the world is far less than the present huge expansion of world population. To compete for an insufficient supply of food is inefficient and can only breed fear and conflict. Already the independence of governments is limited, especially in economic affairs: it looks as if the only hope for a peaceful way of reaching a solution to the problem of an ever expanding world population, which would soon outgrow food and other resources, is a full scale international programme for economic and social development, aimed at raising the quality of living to a level where 'demographic take-off' occurs in order to reduce family size and achieve stable populations.

Some implications for education

Countries of the Third World are characterised in varying degrees by having low standards of living, rapidly increasing populations and incomplete educational systems with many children having no schooling and with widespread illiteracy. Education already takes a major share of the budget in most of these countries, often as much as a fifth, usually more than any other sphere of expenditure; and all too often the aim of expanding the provision of schools becomes no more than a losing race against the rising tide of young children.

The failure of schooling to keep pace with the increase of population is revealed by UNESCO statistics. During the decade between 1960 and 1970 there was an increase in world enrolment for education within the age range 5 to 24 from 324 million in 1960 to 482 million in 1970 (these figures exclude China, North Korea and North Vietnam, which had an estimated enrolment of 150 million). Of this overall increase of 160 million, 100 million were in primary schools. However, the number of children of primary age not enrolled increased during the same period by 165 million. That is, at a period when tremendous efforts were being made to expand primary schooling, the number of children not enrolled was increasing even more rapidly than the number enrolled. Since then the rate of school expansion has declined. There is clearly no prospect of providing schools for all children, at any rate for the next generation or two.

Yet education has an essential part to play in breaking into the vicious circle of rapid population increase preventing development, while development is a necessary condition for reducing the rate of population increase. It follows that the contribution of education to development must involve all children in some appropriate way; not providing schools for some children and nothing for others. A fresh approach is needed.

This raises political issues. The pressure in most Third World countries is for more schools, which offer young people a better chance to develop themselves in the sense of getting a better position in society. This is a very different outlook from an overall approach to social development; and questions about the form society should take are inherently political, depending on national policies. In effect this means that social policy, of which education forms a part, is a matter to be decided by the government of each nation; and this age is one in which the power of nations, and their determination to be 'independent', is as strong as ever, especially those which have escaped recently from colonialism, and certainly much stronger than any international influences. For many years this will continue to be a world of separate nations. Prejudiced and aggressive as nationalism often is, it can also give a unity of political will to nations that are often artificial entities, and a vital sense of self-respect and belonging.

However, many of the problems facing individual nations can only be solved by international cooperation. This applies to most aspects of development, which alone can lead to more stable populations, and critically to present world food problems. Hence the pressure for cooperation grows, while the determination of nations to control their own policies is not diminished; and the clamour for a 'new economic order' emerges out of the paradox.

What has all this to do with education? In the first place, education has to be planned as an integral part of overall development policy. It is not merely concerned with literacy or 'general education', but with contributing to a better standard of living; and in so doing it helps to reduce the rate of population increase to a level that can be better supported. If more food is to be grown, then education should be involved; and similarly if family planning is to be taken seriously, then it also requires a comprehensive approach using all appropriate educational means. Moreover, education has to be much broader than schooling, for many countries cannot provide enough schools for the growing population of children anyway. The outlook must also be wide if it is to encourage both national development and international understanding and cooperation.

Notes

[1] The following books will give a general introduction to population problems:
R. Symonds and M. Carder, *The United Nations and the Population Question*, Chatto and Windus, London, 1973.
S. H. Ominde and C. N. Ejiogu (eds.), *Population Growth and Economic Development in Africa*, Heinemann, London, 1972.
J. Barratt and M. Louw (eds), *International Aspects of Over-Population*, Macmillan, London, 1972.
S. Johnson, *The Population Problem*, David and Charles, Newton Abbot, 1973.
[2] T. E. Smith (ed.), *The Politics of Family Planning in the Third World*, George Allen and Unwin, London, 1973.
P. M. Blake, *Family Planning in India: Diffusion and Policy*, Arnold, London, 1975.
[3] A simple introduction is given by:
E. Stamp, *The Hungry World*, Arnold, Leeds, 1967/revised ed. 1972.

3 Changing Concepts of Educational Development

Emphasis on economic growth

The outlook on educational development was profoundly affected, as we have seen, by the ending of colonialism. This was a long drawn out process, which started at the end of the Second World War, reached its peak in the 1960s, and was almost complete by the mid 1970s. Another powerful influence was the rapid spread of mass communication, as a result of technical advances during the war, and this brought sudden awareness that two-thirds of the world population was desperately poor and on the brink of starvation. In consequence, the first priority in development was to reduce poverty and the widespread risk of famine, with the main emphasis on aid for economic growth to enable the 'underdeveloped' nations, as they were called then, to escape from starvation and raise their standards of living towards those of the advanced nations as quickly as they could. There was much discussion of how the phase of 'economic take-off', using Rostow's terminology (more acceptable in those days than it is now), could be reached; and whether the developing countries could somehow take short cuts to enable them to 'catch up' with the advanced countries. A few countries did achieve rapid economic growth, at any rate for a time, because of a combination of favourable circumstances, although the gains were largely offset by their increase in population. In developing countries, however, economic progress was slow, certainly far slower than in the industrial countries, and a feeling of disillusionment began to spread when it seemed that all the advantages in world trade were with the advanced countries.

Education was regarded as important at this time, especially by the newly independent nations, for several reasons. Their political leaders were under great pressure to provide free primary or basic schooling for all children. This attracted many votes when elections were held in the early days, before nearly all these nations adopted one party or military governments. More important, education was one of the human rights set out in the UN Charter, and the overcoming of ignorance was a necessary means to improving the quality of life. In addition, education was seen as having two more specific aims: to raise the level of skills, especially technical and management skills, needed to support economic growth; and to provide an adequate supply of the whole range of professional expertise needed to run a modern nation, and without which there would be continued dependence on foreign experts. These requirements were worked out using the techniques of manpower planning. The Report of the Ashby Committee on higher education in Nigeria has already been mentioned as an outstanding example of the application of these techniques, which have made a valuable contribution to the planning of vocational education. The forecasts have been useful, within broad limits, in clearly defined fields like the training of doctors, nurses, teachers, agricultural officers, engineers of various kinds etc.; but they are vulnerable to economic fluctuations and other unpredictable changes.

The initial emphasis on economic growth was soon found to have serious weaknesses when taken as an aim by itself, for development is a complex process, in which economic growth is only one of a number of interrelated aspects. This became evident as experience was gained with aid projects.

Education and aid programmes

The early aid projects for developing agriculture, irrigation, industries, transport, etc., were ten years or so later showing very disappointing results. Programmes were subjected to endless delays, a considerable proportion of expenditure seemed to be lost through inefficiency or diverted into the pockets of businessmen, contractors, land owners or administrators; and those who were intended to benefit often gained little. Gradually experience gave a better understanding of the complexity of these operations. Skills were needed at all levels, from those involved in planning and administration to those whom the project was intended to benefit; and this involved an elaborate system of education and training. Much of the initial direction and supervision had to be done by experts from advanced countries while local counterparts were being trained before taking over, and this training programme for key persons had to be supplemented by on-the-job training for everyone involved in the project.

However, the failure was not simply in project planning and control. Two other requirements became evident. The first was the closer integration of projects with overall plans for development; for example, agricultural projects were sometimes dependent on far-reaching reform of laws and customs on land tenure, which might involve a long campaign of public education and protracted legal procedures extending over a number of years. Again, success would depend on coordination with other aspects of development such as transport, storage and marketing of agricultural produce, the development of cooperatives, banking services, etc. The early lessons of the Tennessee Valley Authority about comprehensive planning and overall control of a major development project are still relevant; and the outcome must be economically viable in the long run if it is to improve the standard of living of those whom it is intended to help.

The second requirement came to be understood more slowly. Although aid projects are designed for economic development, their true objective should be to improve, directly or indirectly, the living conditions of human communities; and a social balance sheet in human terms is far more subtle than an economic one, especially when it is concerned not only with persons as individuals, but also with families and communities whose delicate pattern of supportive relationships can be easily disrupted. This raises difficult questions, such as whether the disturbance of a community by planned development will lead to gains that outweigh the losses; and whether the stresses that are inevitably caused can be channelled in support of the development. An illustration can be given by the experience in advanced countries of the problems of rehousing people from slum clearance, when the loss of the accustomed community life has sometimes overshadowed the advantages of better housing. For example, it became clear when much rehousing was done in multistorey blocks of apartments, that the disadvantages were far greater than was anticipated, on adults as well as on children: so much so that in many places it has been decided to build no more of them (in a few places even pull them down).[1] Yet the dislocation of communities involved in many aid projects is much greater. The building of dams and large irrigation schemes may require towns and villages or nomad tribes to be moved to another location, perhaps far away, with very different terrain and climate, and consequent differences in occupations and ways of living. Adjustment to such profound changes is even harder for people with little education. Careful studies by sociologists and anthropologists can help to make the best of the change, but it is difficult to predict what the consequences will be – just as the consequences of moving people from slums to tower blocks were not predicted. In general, sociologists have played only a minor role in planning aid projects, and anthropologists much less. Nor is their contribution an easy one to make, although there have been a number of research studies on the impact of modern civilisation on primitive societies, because the outcome of the interactions in a given situation is difficult to foresee.[2] In practice, however, many of the poor of the Third World live in urban or rural slums, which are characterised by a lack of social organisation and ability to act together for their own improvement: ignorance and fear are their main attributes.

We have distinguished two aspects of education in aid programmes: (i) education to give specific skills e.g. to perform certain jobs in a factory, on a construction project etc.; or, in agriculture, to grow new crops or improve herds, or learn more efficient management; and (ii) education aimed at improving the quality of living of individuals in a community, raising the level of mutual understanding and cooperation, and encouraging the growth of democratic leadership to enable the community to take its own initiatives. Although the situation varies in each project, it is the second of these that often provides the key to sustained development after the initial thrust of the project comes to an end; and this raises at once the question of what kind of society we think should be the aim, and what we mean by 'quality of living'.

Improving the quality of life

There is much debate, in those countries in which freedom of discussion in word and print is allowed, about what form society should take, and what is meant by improving the 'quality of living'. This is not the place to consider in detail the political issues involved, but one or two general comments are relevant.[3]

Most nations of the Third World have one party or military governments of an authoritarian kind. The reasons for this are complex, but they often claim it has advantages in enabling their governments to have tight central control of development planning and execution. However that may be, the trend is obvious, especially in nations which gained their independence in the last decade or two. For example, all the former colonies of Britain and France in Africa, except the Ivory Coast, had two or more political parties at the time of independence, and constitutions on Western European lines, and within ten years every one of them had changed to a one party or military government. In many countires of Asia, the Middle East and South America the basic features of political democracy – representation of the people, freedom of speech in discussion and through mass media, independence of the law and preservation of individual rights, and so on – are poorly represented. However, the great democratic traditions are widely understood, and the struggle to preserve and give them modern expression continues. What has to be admitted is that the political legacy bequeathed to their colonies by Britain, France and other powers, including the USA in the Philippines, has not proved generally acceptable or practicable. Several former British colonies in the West Indies still provide a tenuous exception; and India has maintained a parliamentary form of democracy under leaders of great ability until the restrictions of 1975. Following the USA's withdrawal without honour from Vietnam in 1975, Asia is faced with a spread of communism on similar lines to that which China has developed, although even some of the countries in close proximity to their large neighbour may be as determined as Korea to preserve their own characteristic cultures and develop their own variations on the Chinese doctrines.

The freedom of nations, and of individuals, to make decisions for themselves on a wide range of matters consonant with a more gerneral 'good', are political principles of great importance and are embodied in the ideas of democracy. In addition, however, the notion of 'quality of living' has two other attributes of special significance for the Third World. The first are those human rights incorporated in the UN Charter – the basic rights to adequate food, shelter, clothing, education, work and so on. Without these a person has neither freedom nor self-respect; and the plain fact is that many people – perhaps 500 million – at present lack these minimal requirements. For them political democracy is not the first priority. The second attribute, which comes into play above this minimal level, is that individuals should be members of an equitable society, If this is not so, freedom and self-respect are much diminished. In this respect China has attracted much attention by its achievements; and several Third World nations, notably Cuba, Tanzania and Chile, have adopted strongly socialist forms of government, as we have noted already (though two of these have been influenced more by Russia than China).

The phrase 'quality of living' can be used to denote the opposite of 'deprivation'; and it is well known that deprivation is a relative term. A person who feels deprived in one situation may not in another; while a person who does not feel deprived may change his feeling in this respect on seeing another member of his society get a preferential advantage, such as a large pay increase for no 'good reason'. As we have seen, there is an absolute minimum of basic rights (e.g. of diet as set out by the World Health Organisation) below which 'quality of living' cannot be satisfying; but above that it is relative. This is an important notion underlying the whole concept of development.

The quality of an individual's life, and of the community in which he is living, are intimately related. An aid project may fail because the individuals involved lacked the necessary skills or attitudes; or because the social organisation of the communities involved was inadequate to enable a response to be made to the aid stimulus. We can therefore distinguish two separate, though related, requirements: for the education of individuals to enable them to respond to new opportunities; and for the social development of the community to enable it to respond effectively. Many Third World communities are socially undeveloped, and the first priority may be to improve the social conditions before starting an aid project. Unfortunately the approach through 'community development' or 'social welfare' is often regarded as second best to schooling, and designed to keep people in an inferior position. This is a difficulty which can be overcome by having better development projects, a problem to which we shall return in later chapters.

The notion of 'quality of living' is so fundamental to the concept of development that it may be helpful to summarise the points which have just been made. First, there are basic human needs mentioned in the UN Charter of Human Rights which are a minimal requirement, in the absence of which the idea of 'quality of living' cannot be applied. Second, freedom to make responsible decisions, within broad limits, is a necessary condition for satisfaction and self-respect, both for nations and individuals; and this is related to the principles of democracy. Third, the notion of 'quality of living' is relative, not closely linked with specific physical standards, but more easily satisfied in a reasonably egalitarian society. Fourth, that the notion involves not only individuals, but also the communities in which they live. Even these rough guidelines are not easy to follow in practice. Yet they reflect a much wider approach to the problems of development than in the early days when the emphasis was predominantly on economic growth.

The attractions of industrialisation

A large part of the world's population is living at or below the level of bare subsistence – the estimate is that some 500 million in Third World countries are undernourished or starving. These countries are bound to strive desperately to improve standards of living, and they see little prospect of this through rural development. The evidence of the last twenty or thirty years shows beyond doubt that the industrial nations have had much faster economic growth than the predominantly agricultural nations of the Third World. The gap between rich nations and the majority of the poor ones has grown wider, in spite of all the aid programmes.

The appeal of industrialisation is naturally very strong. It seems to offer the only hope, for any nation without oil or valuable minerals, of rapid economic growth. It could open the way to economic independence, in the sense of not having to import the whole range of industrial products, and from the endless struggles with shortage of foreign exchange that this involves. When raw materials such as bauxite and other minerals are being exported, there is an opportunity to do some refining first, and thus provide a lead in to industrial development. The argument is all the stronger for the fortunate nations with oil, for, apart from exporting it, they can use it as a source of power and raw material from which to start developing petrochemical industries.

There is also a strong, if at times subconscious, appeal because modern society is seen as being essentially technological and urban, and there is a keen desire to be 'modern', as evidenced by the new international airports and fine public buildings in Third World capital cities, all too often rising above a mass of poverty. Industry also has the attraction of expanding the wage earning sector of the population, and of providing new jobs when the rate of full or partial unemployment is generally very high in these countries.

The countries that have achieved the fastest economic growth have all done it through industrialisation, like Japan and West Germany; and without it Russia would have little strength. The few countries that have developed through agriculture, such as Denmark and New Zealand, are the exceptions that prove the rule. But there are great difficulties facing a Third World nation wishing to industrialise – the problems of very large capital investment, labour skills, and the whole complex of associated requirements in modern marketing, transport, communications, banking and other services etc.[4] A complete network of development is required, to provide the infrastructure to support the factories.

The appeal of industrialisation, strong as it is, has recently been tempered by two other considerations. The remarkable economic progress of the advanced industrial countries over the last two or three decades is beginning to be threatened by the heedless waste of resources and by the serious spread of pollution. Japan offers a notable example of very rapid economic development and of severe pollution, which could only be controlled at a greater cost than the country is yet willing to pay. At least as serious is the profligate consumption of limited natural resources, and the danger of accumulating long-life atomic waste.

A more general criticism is gradually influencing world opinion and affecting governments, to the effect that economies based on ever increasing consumption, and on vast production of armaments both for 'defence' and to be sold abroad, are vulnerable to internal pressures and to fluctuating conditions of international trade. The reckless waste of resources and spread of pollution have also begun to threaten the economic progress of the advanced industrial countries. The warnings were suddenly reinforced by the Arab action in using oil as a political sanction, which revealed how vulnerable the advanced industrial economies are. There is a growing question about motives and ideals, as well as about economic uncertainty. For instance, it is the impact of difficulties over international trade that has led to the strange tautomerism of a 'zero-growth economy'. The countries of the Third World join in the questioning and wonder whether they should strive to follow in the footsteps of the industrialised nations. Yet all of them will wish to have at least a limited development of industries, taking advantage of their resources, contributing appropriately to their economies, and relieving the continual shortage of foreign exchange needed for development.

The need for rural development

There can be no doubt that the main thrust for development in Third World countries in which most of the population is rural, should be through agriculture. All the more so when their populations are increasing rapidly, and when the world has just moved into an overall shortage of food in spite of the 'green revolution' and other developments.[5] Yet the difficulties seem to be almost insuperable, for there appears to be a dual imbalance, both economic and social. Even in advanced countries with modern systems of farming, highly mechanised and well financed, it does not seem to be generally profitable: while large commercial and industrial undertakings are heavily taxed, farming often has to be subsidised. Moreover, most people seem to prefer to live in urban conditions, with better facilities for social life, schooling and entertainment, than to live and work in agriculture. Even if the economic balance of advantage could be changed in some way, as it might be, the question of amenities would loom large; and isolation, lack of running water, electricity, etc., are far more acute in the rural communities of the Third World than in advanced countries. While little is known about just what the reasons are – and they are bound to vary from one situation to another – the migration of population from countryside to towns and cities is a widespread phenomenon, occurring in all parts of the world.

Little has been done in the Third World to improve agriculture and rural life, compared with the large visible investment in modernising the cities. Brilliant research in plant breeding has led to new high yielding varieties of rice and wheat, which raised hopes of increasing the world production of food through the 'green revolution'; but the world price of agricultural products has not risen in line with industrial products. There have been many other significant developments, though the prospects have been clouded by the steep rise in the price of fertilisers as a consequence of the large increase in oil prices. Unfortunately rural development depends on a complex of different kinds of factors which are difficult to control, such as land tenure and inheritance, market prices, education in new plant and animal husbandry methods, social changes in village life, rainfall and other aspects of weather, irrigation schemes, improvement of communications, opportunities to gain education beyond primary level, etc. At first sight, it would appear to be much more difficult to achieve agricultural and rural development than to build a factory, and perhaps it is. Yet the dual pressures of population increase and rising unemployment cannot be met in most Third World countries by industrialisation, and rural development is crucial for their future. What stands out clearly is that a broad and coordinated approach is essential for rural development, and that education has to be integrated with it.

Point

The cultural diversity of nations

In spite of the modern wonders of instant news and rapid travel, the peoples of the world continue to live in an almost unbelievable variety of cultural settings, so complex that few can learn to understand more than a fragment of them in a lifetime. As the earliest races of man slowly spread in pockets across the continents, mingling and interbreeding, developing language and starting agriculture and settlements, forming the great empire civilisations of Persia, Greece and Rome, and spreading the world religions of Christianity, Islam and Hinduism, so the present extraordinary mosaic of cultures evolved. It is still a world of many nations, whose relationships have been suddenly transformed by the developments of modern technology in the last few decades which impinge on them all in different ways: the atom bomb and mass destruction, antibiotics, transistors and instant news, the computer and automated industry, the economic power of international trading and so on. Their influence quickly circles the globe and helps to shape the international scene, but they do not radically change the human context in which the vast majority of the world population carry on their daily lives. For many, indeed most, their lives are coloured by poverty, ill health, ignorance; and characterised by their language, family and social customs, religion, traditions, occupations – what can be described as the 'culture' in which they live. There may be a rich literature or little; a strong all-pervading religious influence, or primitive animism; vivid traditions of song, dance and drama as part of a satisfying life in community or tribe – the variety of cultural patterns is almost infinite, though a number of main themes can be discerned. One of these is the cultural setting in which a child grows up, and through which his personality is formed, and on which he will always be dependent even though he may, with the help of 'education', grow beyond its limitations. If education ignores this background, it can only be disruptive or barren, though it should also be ready to open windows on to the wider world beyond the local scene.

The great movements of people and ideas that have shaped the cultural patterns of the world do not coincide with the present boundaries of nations.

Some nations are small in area or population, the smallest hardly larger in population than a market town. Others are very large. China is the nation with the largest population, over 786 million (at mid–1972), in an area of the same size as the USA; India has over 563 million in a relatively small sub-continent; Russia is a federation with a total population of more than 247 million, occupying a fifth of the world's land surface; while the USA has over 208 million in half a continent. Thus there is a tremendous range of variation between nations in population, area of land and other physical attributes. The variation is at least as great in the constituent races, religions, languages etc., each having its unique and characteristic composition; and a majority of them being plural societies.

Thus a nation which decides educational policy through its central government is often a plural society, embracing different cultures, religions, races or tribes, and yet seeking to make its education a strong force for nation building. This tends to place the main emphasis on the unifying power of education rather than on its close association with local or regional cultures: the pressure is for a single national language and for a common culture to ensure national unity – whereas many nations are artificial in terms of culture, often the accidental products of colonial history or past wars.

Yet nationalism still commands strong loyalty, as much in the advanced countries as in the developing ones, and by encouraging pride in the present and past history, arts, literature etc., it gives the peoples of a nation a satisfying sense of belonging and of self respect.[6] In many countries there was an ancient indigenous culture to serve this purpose, notably in the Middle East and Asia. In others a new social or political philosophy was needed, like the cult of négritude developed by Leopold Senghor to foster pride in being black, and to overcome the sense of inferiority induced by the French culture which dominated Senegal. His poetry, and the extensive literature now being created by younger negro writers from West Africa and other parts of the continent, helped to develop a feeling of national self-esteem during the struggles for independence and subsequently. This not only enriched the cultural background of education in those countries, but also gave confidence to break away from inherited school systems in an effort to create something more indigenous and closer to national aims for development. By strengthening their own sense of nationhood, gaining pride in their own history and culture, the developing countries are becoming ideologically less dependent on the industrial technology of the advanced nations and its associated modern culture, more hesitant about the social disruption that seems to go with rapid technological advance, and more inclined to consider new approaches.

It is not simply a question of the developing countries shaking themselves free from the dominance of the advanced countries, for the latter are themselves going through a traumatic questioning of accepted cultural values. In universities and in the intellectual climate generally there is a progressive expansion and fragmentation of knowledge, and a loss of cultural identity as the traditional orthodoxies are steadily undermined. The comment has been made by Richard Hoggart and others that the present turmoil may arise from the erosion of the Protestant ethic in its two main forms of expression: its attitude to competitive work and to sexual life. In its place there is growing a more insistent egalitarianism, challenging the meritocratic society, yet anxious to assert individual freedom and responsibility. This change involves a continuing reinterpretation of the great democratic traditions, and the context in which it has to be expressed is a constraining economic one, which bears most heavily on the poor nations of the Third World. They are bound to be influenced by the confused cultural questioning of the advanced nations; but they find no generally accepted unifying framework of knowledge or beliefs, or of values in art of literature, to follow, and are left to create their own cultural identity. This may seem far removed from problems of development, but it is close to any consideration of 'qualities of living'.

Education as an integral part of development

The main emphasis in the 1950s and 1960s was, as we have seen, on economic growth to enable the poor nations with a large part of their population at bare subsistence level or below to raise their standard of living. This is certainly an essential aspect of development, but it proved to be far too narrow as an objective. Most people in the low income countries suffer from miserably poor food, housing, health and other physical conditions, and also live in socially undeveloped conditions with poor community life, especially in urban and rural slums. This calls for a more comprehensive and integrated policy for development.

When so large a proportion of the world's population is on the brink of starvation, economic growth remains of prime importance. However, the gap between the rich industrial nations and the poor agricultural countries has grown wider over the last two decades, and there has been little prospect of improvement without industry. The balance of trade may change, as an outcome of the oil crisis, in favour of primary producers. Nevertheless, most Third World countries wish to have some industrial development, both for economic growth and employment and to secure their independence. This requires a supporting base of technical education at appropriate levels; and all nations also wish to educate their own administrators, professionals and specialists of all kinds.

b) But few Third World countries can rely on industrial growth for their developments (perhaps only city–ports like Singapore and Hong Kong). For most of them the future depends, of necessity, on rural development, and this in turn depends on better living conditions and amenities as well as improved agriculture to bring higher earnings. Moreover, rural development holds the keys to reducing the size of families – and population control has become a vital issue on a world scale and for many of these nations – and to preventing a further rise in unemployment; and education on appropriate lines would have to play an integral role in achieving the necessary transformation.

c) The 'modern sector', with its advanced education and the accompanying way of life, can only be for a small minority in the Third World. Most people will live in a much simpler, more traditional way, and education should be one of the means through which this can be made satisfying. If a poor country is to be independent in any real sense in the modern world, it must have a minority of highly educated persons, and a majority attuned to a much simpler condition of living, and an education to match. The concept of development has to embrace several levels, with coordinated social and economic aims. As a goal, this is profoundly different from the present situation in many countries, where the basic schooling for all children – or as many as can be afforded – is essentially a preparation for the fierce competition for selection for secondary schooling, and that in turn for college or university. It is a system designed for the very few who succeed, and either unsuited or harmful for the majority.

Thus the concept of development which twenty or thirty years ago had its focus on economic growth and the expansion of formal education, has now become much broader in scope, involving aspects which can be described as productive, democratic and humanistic. Production is closely related to economic growth, and will sometimes pull in opposite directions from the last two, which are innately egalitarian and concerned with human development. The urge for democracy is as strong as was the opposition to colonialism, and it affects the whole of society; for the individual should find satisfaction in his family and community, at work, in freedom of discussion, participation in political activities, recreation, travel etc.

This is a much wider and more complex notion of development, and much harder to strive towards; and it still requires conditions of living appreciably above mere subsistence, so that the economic core of the problem remains. Moreover, in the Third World these aims have to be realised in societies that are widely extended in standards of living and education, and divided between rural and urban industrial ways of life. Hence the need for a concept of balanced development for extended societies, and for appropriate forms of democratic government, whether strongly socialist or more open. It is an

42

advantage that many developing countries have strengthened their own sense of nationhood, gaining pride in their own history and culture, and in consequence becoming more ideologically independent. As part of this broader outlook, education can be seen as a vital strand in national development for a 'better life', entwined with all the aspects of interpreting and seeking to express what this involves in economic, social and political terms.

Notes

[1] Pearl Jephcott, *Homes in High Flats*, Oliver and Boyd, London, 1972.

[2] M. Mead, *New Lives for Old: Cultural Transformation – Manus 1928–1953*, Morrow, New York, 1953 (and later eds.).

[3] Dom Moraes, *A Matter of People*, Praeger, New York, 1974.

[4] An introduction to economic aspects of development is given by: P. Streeten, *The Frontiers of Development Studies*, Macmillan, London, 1972. C. A. Anderson and M. J. Bowman, *Education and Economic Development*, Aldine, Chicago, 1965.

[5] K. Griffin, *The Political Economy of Agrarian Change – An Essay on the Green Revolution*, Macmillan, London, 1974.

[6] Ezekiel Mphahlele, *The African Image*, Faber, London, 1974. J. Ayodele Langley, *Pan-Africanism and Nationalism in West Africa 1900–1945*, Oxford University Press, London, 1973.

4 Problems of Educational Development

The economic constraints on education

We have seen how the outlook on educational development has changed from regarding it as the expansion of an organised system of schools, colleges and universities, to being an integral part of overall development. The cost of education, like other social services, falls on government – the elimination of fees is far more necessary in poor countries than rich ones, where fees at a variety of levels are often charged for tertiary education. National income can for this purpose be expressed by the Gross National Product, and Third World countries have by definition a low GNP per head of the population. Since the 'oil crisis' of late 1973, the Third World has been polarised more sharply into three groups in terms of their economic growth potentials:

1 'Fast growth' countries, those which export oil or minerals, with combined populations of about 400 million, i.e. 20 per cent of the two billion in the developing countries according to World Bank estimates.
2 'Moderate growth' countries, now in the middle and upper categories of developing countries, having per capita incomes over $200 a year, and with reasonable prospects for moderate long term growth; with about 600 million population.
3 'Negative growth' countries, formerly with low rates of growth having per capita incomes below $200 a year, and affected very adversely by the 'oil crisis'; with a population of about one billion.

This categorisation has immediate implications for education. Group 1 is already modernising rapidly, and group 2 slowly. But group 3 has no prospect of modernisation, even though terms of trade may move in their favour if prices of agricultural products rise, and inflation slows down in the advanced countries; for they cannot provide capital for investment internally, nor attract it from the outside, on anything like the immense scale needed. Aid programmes help, although these are largely offset by rapid population increase in many of these countries. The outlook is clear, however: their future will have to depend on rural development and not on the 'modern' sector. That is, for nearly all the population of the group 3 countries, and for many in group 2, the key to the future lies in rural development. This applies to around 70 per cent of the total of two billion in the developing countries. These countries will not be able to provide schools for all their children, and they are bound to develop education along other lines. Although no wise person makes prophecies lightly, it can be said that there is no indication at present of their condition being likely to improve for at least another generation. Incomes are at present below $200 a person, and the forecast by the World Bank is that their GNP per capita will decline in 1974–80, while all others will rise. This is hardly a situation likely to attract foreign investment on a large scale. The development of these countries therefore presents an urgent challenge.[1]

The cost of primary schooling is relatively high in these low income developing countries of group 3 because the salaries of teachers are high in relation to the GNP per capita, which is itself very low; and this is so even though the standard of education is far below that of schools in advanced countries, in terms of facilities, attainments and scope of the curriculum. Taking Mali as an example, the cost per pupil a year of primary education is 16,000 Mali francs, and the average income a head is 40,000 Mali francs. That is, primary education costs about 40 per cent of the average income. In Latin America and Asia the figure is about 10 per cent, still impossibly high for universal schooling when the income level is so low. In Western Europe comparable figures are about 6 per cent for France, 9 per cent for Britain and nearly 20 per cent for Scandinavia.

There is another difficulty seen in an acute form in some former colonial countries in Africa. In most advanced countries, and generally in Latin America and Asia, a teacher gets on average between three and five times the national income; but in Africa it may be as much as twenty-five times higher. This is a legacy of former colonial days, when the salaries of expatriate administrators and teachers were linked with their home countries, and these salaries were taken over by the local persons as they replaced the expatriates before and after independence. In consequence, civil servants, including teachers, have disproportionately high salaries, as well as security of tenure, which makes them a very privileged group occupying between one-third and two-thirds of the small wage earning sector of between 1 per cent and 5 per cent of the working population. Naturally this privileged group is in a sufficiently strong position to oppose moves to reduce the differentials appreciably. What is even more serious, the schools were developed along Western European lines to produce just these civil servants, including teachers; and with expansion the schools produce a surplus for whom there are no jobs. In consequence there is much unemployment and frustration, and a dearth of young people with a suitable education for the large rural or small industrial

46

sectors. The present schools teach the wrong attitudes and skills, and are divorced from the indigenous cultures – a situation that is acute in Africa, and occurs to a varying extent in other developing countries. The significance of this for the present discussion, however, is that not only is it wrong for development, it simply cannot be afforded.

In spite of the difficulties even the poorest states will be determined to have a small modern sector to provide the apparatus of government, diplomatic representation, etc. Hence these countries usually have a small modern sector and a large low income population, mostly rural but also accumulating in urban slums. The problem for education is to have one system which will provide for both these very different needs; and how this could be developed depends on the system of education that exists already.

Variations in the present educational provision

There is a surprising range of extremes in the educational systems of different developing countries, as can be illustrated by the following broad categories:

1   Countries with a very small educational base, so small as to make development difficult, exemplified by the large, sparsely populated countries of Middle Africa.
2   Countries with a wide educational and cultural base. The main limiting factor for development is not lack of education, but the social structure; a situation characteristic of Latin America.
3   Countries with a surfeit of educated people in a population too large for the land and other resources, such as India and Pakistan.

The contribution which education can make to development evidently differs in fundamental respects in each of these groups, although they represent no more than rough and ready divisions to clarify the main issues. They could not serve as a basis for development planning, but they highlight the contrasts in the educational problems between one country and another.[2]

In the first group, the shortage of educated and trained people constitutes a serious barrier to development, and the expansion of education is a priority task. At best the process of expansion is slow, working up through the successive age levels, and dependent on a large, and costly, increase in the number of teachers. If they are to make reasonable progress, low income countries need substantial financial assistance and the help of specialists from abroad. Examples would include countries such as Mauritania on the north west of Africa, Mali, Niger and Chad in the sub-Sahara belt, the Central African Republic and Zaire. There is a dual need: for a broad expansion of rural education as part of coordinated programmes of rural development, and the provision of a small system of formal education to provide administrators, teachers and specialists of many kinds – there are arguments in favour of doing some education at university level in the country, while sending specialists for training abroad in advanced science and technology and certain other fields where the numbers are small. These dual needs are bound to lead to a polarisation of the educational provision, in kind as well as in level. This development can take place almost *de novo* in these countries with little education, in the sense that it does not have to break into a resistant established system. In most of these countries in Africa there are fair prospects for rural development, as long as it can be adjusted to low and uncertain rainfall and other adverse natural conditions.

The countries of the second group already have an educated élite with a wide cultural base, giving a sufficiency of administrators, teachers, members of the professions, entrepreneurs, etc., for development. An expansion of primary schooling would be desirable, but what holds it back is the resistance of the social structure, and the political domination of the élite that is associated with it. Although the situation varies from one country in Latin America to another, and fluctuates with political and economic change, yet economic progress generally favours the privileged group who themselves contribute little to the advancement, and the impoverished masses gain little if at all. This seems to be the main cause of tensions and of the activities of the urban guerillas, although there are other contributory reasons in situations that are often confused as well as complex. The regressive social dominance is exercised by combinations of landowners, families with inherited wealth, the army, the church and the swollen bureaucracies, sometimes in association with foreign influence through multinational companies. The sad story of Allende's rise and fall in Chile has already been mentioned. Cuba has struggled successfully to preserve its social revolution. Mexico has moved ahead after breaking by revolution the dominations of its landowners. Brazil provides a different example, with about the highest economic growth rate in the world, under an authoritarian military regime, with an ambitious economic development policy, and at the same time continuing widespread illiteracy. In a situation as complex as this, when the present educational system with all its many limitations is sufficient for rapid economic progress, it may be that an extension of education would serve a different purpose in preparing the way for a more democratic social and political organisation. This is particularly so when endemic inflation in these countries usually hurts the poor most, and they can do least to soften its impact. A different example is provided by Haiti, which has been under despotic rule since the French were expelled 150 years ago. Little changed by outside influence under a régime that has recently been relaxed, it is a backward society, with relatively few tensions – in contrast to neighbouring Jamaica, which has become an increasingly violent society while seeking vigorously, under able democratic leadership, to modernise.

The third group refers especially to India, Pakistan and Bangladesh, though some of its features can be seen in other parts of Asia. The educational systems are highly developed, giving an overproduction of teachers, administrators, entrepreneurs, even scientists and doctors, who are generally in short supply in the Third World. There is an ancient and still influential cultural base. The political systems have been largely democratic, though more so in India than Pakistan, for the power of the hierarchical rulers and large landowners was ended, or very greatly reduced, at independence and in later reforms. The limitations to development are twofold: populations far beyond the available land and capital, and continuing high rates of population increase. The large and relentlessly increasing populations are the product of historical factors which have operated for a long time and cannot be easily changed, as recent efforts at family planning have shown. The gains in opening up large areas of new arable land through irrigation, and improved methods of crop and animal husbandry, have been offset by the population growth, which overwhelms efforts to raise living standards: a situation which has applied equally in Egypt. The problem is how to break into the vicious circle of poverty and high fertility, when the latter will not decline until living standards are seen to rise, while improvement in living standards awaits a decline in fertility. There seems to be no short cut: the only hope lies in a coordinated policy for rural development, and to make this really effective would require a radical improvement of rural living conditions sufficient to encourage higher production of food, reduce the level of fertility, and maintain the population on the land, preventing the continued exodus which forms the spreading canker of urban slums. But the present system of education does little or nothing to encourage rural development. If there were to be the kind of transformation that appears to be essential for future development, then education would have to undergo a profound change in order to play a key role in the transformation; whereas the present educational system is perpetuating a deep rooted imbalance. Even so, it has to be remembered that India has survived nearly twenty years of independence as a democracy, in spite of its poverty and its astonishing variety of race, culture and language, because many of its people are educated. This makes possibly the vitality of its public life, and its ability to undertake complex development projects. The balance sheet of its inflated educational system has a strong credit side as well as the debits. What is needed is not less education, but different forms of education.

Social change through education

Education contributes to social change at several levels – family and community, as well as in the wider structure and relationships of society; and also in other far-reaching respects, such as the education of girls and women. In this short section, it will only be possible to illustrate some of these aspects, without considering them in detail.

In most undeveloped societies an individual has a clearly defined position in a web comprising his family, an extensive network of kinship, age groups, tribal loyalties, etc. in accordance with traditional customs and rituals. The upbringing of the young is well adapted to continuing the accustomed way of life, and there is no need for schooling in a formal sense to develop literacy or to encourage new ideas and practices. Its virtue is to be supportive, and close to the natural environment, and not to be, in our terms, innovative: the stress is on conformity to accepted customs, and not, as a rule, on individual competitiveness. In the tribal situation communities are small, but such features may be carried over in societies organised on a larger scale. Even in traditional societies without extensive kinship patterns, families are usually large; and this is especially true of Moslem societies, in which a man may have up to four wives provided he can maintain them adequately. What we are considering as 'development' alters the social context, and brings changes, sometimes gradually so that there is time for the old to be assimilated to some extent with the new, at other times quickly enough to cause disruption.

Apart from the question of how fast the changes come about, however, the introduction of a modern sector, with industry and foreign technology, and related expansion of urban living, tends to break the traditional ties of family and kinship and the old hierarchies. The tendency is to move towards a wage earning economy in which the family depends on the wage earner, and does not function as a producing unit. The wage earner is normally a man who is both head of the family and the source of its income. The consequences of this change from the family as a cooperative production unit to the family dependent on its male wage earner is all the more drastic in matrilineal societies (in Ghana, for example, the market women engage in trade, accumulate capital and own property); but it also profoundly affects the position of women in society, the respect of young persons for the old, and so on. Hence many Third World countries are faced with difficult social transitions in moving to an industrial economy, with its inherent pressures towards the urbanised, isolated, nuclear family characteristic of advanced industrial societies. These trends are irresistible in the modern sectors, but they affect only a small minority in developing countries, and most of the population will continue to live in more traditional rural communities. It is evident that both educational provision and social organisation will have to cover a much wider range of conditions than occur in advanced countries.

Under tribal conditions each individual – the young, old, sick, widowed etc. – is cared for within the extended system of family and kinship, though the customs which regulate how this should be done vary greatly from one tribe to another. This characteristic remains in many developing countries, especially in rural areas, and laps over into urban communities which often have a steady flow of people moving to and from the countryside. Each person in this network also has a responsibility to help others, and a man who is rich has a large circle to support, and to give personal help and advice. When he gains a position of responsibility in a modern job in administration, a profession, or in commerce or industry, he naturally carries over the duty to help his kin. The borderline between this and nepotism is not always easy to define. Similarly, the practice of trading exists in all communities, and of paying those who help with introductions or contracts; on a smaller scale it is 'tipping' or 'backsheesh' on a larger scale it is termed 'commission'. Again the dividing line between this and dishonest practice may be hazy, and the present conventions and laws of advanced countries on these matters have evolved through long struggles. But when the practice leads to bribery and corruption on a large scale by those in positions of authority and responsibility in a developing country, it can, and sometimes does, lead to a devastating canker throughout society that undermines its ethical standards and its stability. For when democracy is restricted, those who suffer most will find their only outlet in violence; and when the army is in control, peaceful change is unlikely. It would be entirely wrong to think that these problems have been happily resolved in the advanced countries – the sad story of Nixon, and less elevated examples in other countries, give convincing evidence that this is not so. The developing countries will have to face this problem far more quickly than the advanced countries did, and build up standards of efficiency and honesty in their governments and administration, as many of them have, if the complex processes involved in development are not to break down. But it cannot be expected to happen overnight.

There are acute problems of social change at a more personal level, as well as those at a national level of which we have just been considering one aspect. The loosening of family and kinship relationships leaves an individual in an isolated and exposed position, for which he is unprepared. He does not have the self confidence to 'go it alone', nor the chance to make new and satisfying personal relationships. If he is fortunate to earn a wage in a factory or office, the question of creating a new kind of family life in the strange setting presents many difficulties; and it is unusual, when factories are erected, to build the housing and amenities to create communities in support of the new industries. There are often new industrial estates – of factories – but rarely new balanced communities for working and living. In consequence, the social transition is not helped, and personality can easily be eroded. Yet, when conditions in the countryside offer little or no hope, the young are bound to move to the towns, even if it is only to the growing urban slums. Then, if there is no job, or only occasional opportunities to earn a little money – and it is estimated that a fifth of the population of Third World countries are in this situation – one cannot be surprised that it leads to frustration, crime and violence. The worst effects of unemployment can be more readily absorbed in rural communities, provided they are well above subsistence level; but in towns and cities the consequences are bound to be destructive to society and the individual.

Social change has very different implications in the contrasting conditions of rural development and urban modernisation in the Third World. In the former the task is in general to create new communities, more productive, viable and satisfying; and this involves planned development, which cannot be initiated and carried through without help from outside – usually from the government with bilateral or multilateral foreign aid. Urban modernisation is also susceptible to planning in part, but it is largely shaped by the nation's political views. There is a basic difference between the modern cities of the USA, Canada and Australia, for example, which have grown up on a free enterprise, market directed economic policy, and in which personal achievement is encouraged; and cities of the communist nations which are dominated by the pervasive bureaucracies of the one party government, and the enclosing social pressures for conformity, to which the schools are finely tuned. This represents inevitably an oversimplification, and many cities mix the features of the two extremes just depicted. Moreover, all cities are heavily influenced by the consequences of modern technology, which is the source of industrial growth, with its proliferating international relationships. There is depressing evidence of this sameness in the architecture of new factories and office blocks in cities all over the world – the dull cultural uniformity of modern technology, administration and commerce, which has suffocated the underlying indigenous cultures, and undermined the social relationships that formed a satisfying human environment. However, there is an intermingling below the surface of old and new in any large city in Latin America, Asia, Africa or even in Japan, where industrialisation has been most rapid.

Much has been written about 'culture shock' and the conflict and tensions aroused when a society is subjected to rapid dislocating changes. A few instances have also been described where an isolated primitive society suddenly brought under the influence of an advanced technological society has been able to adapt without disruptive stress. Little is known about the dynamics of the complex social interactions involved; but it is evident that the process may comprise intermingling and adaptation, and not necessarily social breakdown and conflict. An important question is whether education can assist the process of assimilation more actively than by simply providing a common, more or less neutral, school curriculum for all children.

One more feature may be referred to briefly, namely that many Third World nations are plural societies, and this adds a further dimension to problems of development. Many advanced nations also have sharp difficulties on this count, notably the USA with its expanding minority of negroes. Where the Third World suffers more acutely is when this problem is compounded with others in the process of rapid modernisation. It is a theme that colours many of the problems of development, for example in Latin America.

The education of women

Social changes naturally involve women as much as men. Indeed they are more affected because their position in developing countries is generally so much inferior to men. They have to feed the family, fetch water and firewood, look after the home, work in the fields, and market the produce, in addition to bearing and bringing up a long series of children. The tasks allotted to women are those with low status; and any improvement in the way she feeds the family or brings up the children tends to reinforce her traditional role. Most of the low income societies of Asia, Africa and Latin America are male dominated, the woman's place is in the home, and she does the man's bidding. The market women of Ghana and Nigeria are an exception, but in varying degrees women are nearly always subservient to men. This is even more true in Moslem countries, where girls are kept at home after puberty, and a woman may not go out except to market, and then veiled so that no man can look at her face.

In developing countries, as in advanced ones, a subtle inculcation of roles from early childhood builds up the woman's sense of dependence on man. Since the beginning of this century this attitude has been challenged by women in the advanced countries with growing vigour. Slowly they have moved out of domestic service, nursing and teaching, and into many occupations formerly reserved for men. Gradually the notion of 'equal pay for equal work' is being accepted; and the women's rights before the law are being steadily moved nearer to equality with men. These changes have been slow

c

even in societies where schooling has long been provided for girls equally with boys. In the developing countries the changes will inevitably also take a long time, for attitudes deeply rooted in a culture only change slowly.

A much smaller proportion of girls than boys go to school in those developing countries which have not been able to provide universal primary schooling; and where this has been developed, the girls leave earlier, fewer go on to secondary schools, and fewer still to higher education. Better education for girls does bring a change of attitudes, and the gradual opening of new horizons, though change is slow unless education is associated with a wider process of development.

The UN designated 1975 as International Women's Year, following on 1974 which was World Population Year, with the goals of advancing the status of women and encouraging responsible parenthood. At present the vast majority of women in the Third World live in poverty, squalor, ill health and ignorance, quite unable to improve the condition of themselves or their families. It is the woman who must be helped if there is to be improvement in diet, health, infant care and the upbringing of children. She represents half the task in family planning – or less, as long as the man is dominant, and he maintains the feelings of 'machismo', and she the pride of having a baby at breast or slung on her back. At least the advantages of better child spacing should be understood as clearly by the mother as the father. Her improved knowledge of nutrition and hygiene will improve the health of the family; and, if she is literate, she will be more concerned over the education of her children. Yet in spite of courageous efforts by the few educated women in many developing countries, and the sustained efforts of UNICEF (and of the UN Children's Fund, and the UN Fund for Population Activities), there has been little progress. This only serves to reveal how deep-rooted are the instincts and attitudes that perpetuate the subservient position of women in society. To read accounts of the conditions of their lives, so wretchedly and hopelessly deprived, whether in Asia, Africa or Latin America, is profoundly disheartening. There is no avoiding the conclusion that the main hope for improvement lies in overall development programmes.

This conclusion was reinforced, as we saw earlier, by the outcome of the UN Population Conference of 1974 in Bucharest where the notion of population control as a means to development was overwhelmingly opposed, and family planning was given only qualified support as an aspect which a nation might include within a development programme, the stress being firmly placed on more aid to the Third World for development. This may have been in part an irrational response at a political level, deliberately ignoring uncomfortable demographic statistics. But it corresponds with the findings of research that women in low income societies have not only a deep natural instinct for procreation, but also have two other compelling reasons – the desire to have sons, on which their status often largely depends; and the desire for large families, in the hope that the surviving children will provide security for them in their old age. Moreover, in rural societies at a low level of subsistence, children contribute to the family by their labour, and require little more than their food. Not surprisingly, experience has shown that family planning makes little or no headway until the standard of living is raised to a level where infant mortality is reduced, and security for old age is improved, and then it can have a significant effect. Education has not only to be part of development, but it has to be directed to women at least equally with men, and focused not only on literacy but directly on questions of nutrition, hygiene, family planning and so on. If there is to be a levelling off in the increase of world population, that also gives urgency to the education of girls and women.

Education in developing countries with divergent rural and urban societies

We have seen that the concept of education has broadened in recent years. The earlier emphasis on economic growth aimed at improving standards of living, especially of the millions in developing countries who are at bare subsistence level. However, it is now realised that to raise their general standard of living so that they can become more productive is only one phase of development; for concurrently there must be an improvement in the environment for living. This will open the way for a reduction in population increase, which continually offsets all efforts to improve living conditions. This has led to more attention to the notion of 'quality of living', which comprises physical requisites, such as adequate food, shelter, clothing, conditions of health, etc.; conditions to allow individual development, such as education, freedom to enjoy democratic rights, etc.; and a rich social life in a community environment forming part of a just and reasonably egalitarian society.[3] These are only rough expressions of profound questions about human life in a modern society, and they should be qualified in cultural, religious, multiracial and other respects.

Many others have written in the past on this theme. Among them Goulet gives an eloquent description of three universal goals for human life.[4] They are 'life-sustenance', that is the provision of material needs; 'esteem', or self respect among one's fellows; and 'freedom' from servitude to nature, ignorance, other men etc. These are the goals for which one strives in the process of development. They are similar for rich and poor nations, except that the former have the material capacity to meet them (though not the political or moral will to do so for all members of the nation), while the latter do not.

A consideration of 'development' along these lines, however difficult, is close to actual needs in the Third World, but it represents a profound change of approach. The average gross national product per person in a country, or the calories in the average person's diet, are still important, especially at subsistence level. But above that 'quality of living' is relative, depending on individual freedom, rich community life, abundant opportunities for learning, and so on: satisfying conditions can occur in different ways in different situations, and at very different economic levels. In so far as this is true, it should be possible to provide satisfying conditions of living not only in affluent modern suburbs, but equally in the rural communities of low income developing countries. If this objective can be achieved on a much larger scale than has been possible as yet, and if it were to lead to a general stabilising of populations, then it would open up new horizons for development.

This question of 'quality of living' in relation to development is important because, when the economic constraints on education were considered at the beginning of this chapter, it became clear that, while some developing countries could have more or less rapid economic growth, others have the prospect of none. Rapid economic growth enables countries to expand their modern industrial and urban sector. But the future for the countries with no prospect of economic growth, which together have a quarter of the world's population, rests almost entirely on rural development, with only a small governing and administrative modern sector. The educational requirements for these two kinds of society are quite different.

Developing countries differ as much from one another in the extent of development of their systems of schooling as they do in their prospects for economic growth; but there is no correlation between the two, because the interrelationships are evidently complex. Again, there are wide variations in social structure, independent of the other features. Hence there can be no simple model for development in the Third World, and the position of each country has to be analysed in terms of the interaction of the economic, political, social, educational and other complexities; and these must include such aspects as race, religion, language and other cultural differences. As we have seen, one country may need an expansion of formal primary and secondary schooling, like Mali or Zaire; while another low income country may have an overdeveloped system of formal education, which fails to meet the needs of its large rural population, as in India. Some of the problems of the divergent needs of rural and urban development will be considered in relation to particular countries in the next two chapters.

Notes

[1] Address to the Board of Governors of the World Bank by R. S. McNamara, 30 September 1974, World Bank, Washington, 1974.

[2] J. K. Galbraith, *The Underdeveloped Country*, Canadian Broadcasting Council, Toronto, 1965.

[3] A. Curle, *Education for Liberation*, Tavistock, London, 1973.

[4] D. Goulet, *The Cruel Choice*, Atheneum, New York, 1971.

5 Rural Education: Problems and Examples

Past neglect and present goals

The main target for development during the first two decades after the Second World War was directed towards industrialisation and the modern urban sector. The rapid economic growth of the advanced nations was achieved through industrialisation, and in the eyes of the developing nations this modern sector represented 'progress'. In contrast, rural communities were stagnant, and agricultural improvement did not run ahead of population growth, except in a few instances where conditions were transformed by irrigation or better crop or animal husbandry and marketing. There were many wise words spoken by colonial powers about the need for schools to encourage agriculture and an interest in rural life, but the miserable story of school gardens shows how these weak efforts could never get anywhere near the roots of the problems of rural development. The extreme difficulty of organising change in scattered groups of impoverished families seemed overwhelming: they were too poor, ignorant and sick to risk the unknown hazards of changing from their traditional ways. The enlightened village development in India, which sought to revitalise life for the mass of peasants in the countryside, giving it a new spiritual vigour and richness of culture, failed to overcome the deeply engrained resistances – even under the leadership of Gandhi, certainly one of the great men of this century, Tagore and many others. Little wonder that hopes of progress through rural development faded away; especially as China was struggling in turmoil with its revolutionary changes behind closed doors.

Hence the Third World sought economic growth through the development of industry, and social progress through the expansion of the school system to provide wider opportunities for young people, hoping also that better education would bring improvements in society. We have seen how these illusions were shattered. The developing countries could not afford education for all on the model of the advanced countries, and it led to a growing imbalance in society and increasing unemployment of the young on leaving school. Moreover, the great majority of their peoples lived in a rural environment, and would go on doing so. Therefore the challenge of rural develop-

59

ment could not be evaded, however difficult and complex the changes would have to be. The approach of community development, which was rejected by colonial countries on independence as being a second-rate substitute for proper schooling, slowly returned to the scene. The growing threat of unemployment, and the tide of migration to the urban slums, for which industrialisation could not provide a sufficient answer, gave a new sense of urgency to rural development.

For some time the development of the countryside was almost synonymous with improving agricultural output, to which agriculturalists and the Food and Agricultural Organisation of the United Nations had devoted great efforts. But a broader outlook was expressed in the aims of the UN Second Development Decade, which saw rural education not just as agricultural and economic development, with emphasis on an equitable spread of benefits. The goals included more equitable use of arable land and distribution of income; associated improvements in nutrition, housing and health; much better opportunities through education for individual growth and self-fulfilment, with a greater share in decisions affecting their own lives. Improving agricultural productivity was still the key to progress, but depended in turn on all the conditions affecting the lives of farmers, especially peasant farmers.

The priority now being given to agriculture is illustrated by the increase in its share of World Bank lending from 6 per cent during 1948–60 to 24 per cent in 1973–74, with a planned further increase to fifteen billion dollars for 1975–79, of which about half would be for agriculture and half for rural development. As the Bank is the largest source of funds for agriculture in developing countries, its policy on ways to improve the economic and social life of the poor, reviewing the extent and nature of rural poverty and suggesting programmes for rural development, will have wide influence.[1] A pity that the policy is set out in a 'sector paper', for rural development should not be viewed from independent sectors. The tendency is for the approach to be predominantly economic, allied with agriculture under the auspices of FAO, divisions which occur in the United Nations and also in nearly all governments; and this militates against a truly comprehensive approach to rural development. Similarly there is a natural tendency for UNESCO, being representative of governments, to give much attention to formal education, the main responsibility of their Ministries of Education, and to be little concerned with informal and non-formal education.

The outlook on rural development has been greatly influenced by extensive research on theories of economic growth. Much less research has been done on theories of social development, least of all in the area where the anthropological study of undeveloped societies overlaps with sociology; and this is an

60

area of research closely related to education in these societies. Yet, if rural development is to be as much concerned with satisfying 'qualities of living' – as with economic growth, much more than just nutrition, hygiene etc. – then there is an urgent need for more study of what this implies. It is a serious question whether there should not be less talk of 'cost-benefit' analysis and 'management techniques', and much more flexible and sensitive study of what particular rural communities can themselves envisage as improving the quality of their lives – remembering that feelings of satisfaction and respect may be more important than things which can be readily measured, even though they have a much less 'scientific' appearance.

The failure of formal education

The failure is both quantitative and qualitative. The statistics prepared by UNESCO and other agencies giving school enrolments by age and sex in urban and rural areas show several features. First, enrolments are commonly much higher in urban than rural areas, and relatively lower for girls, especially in rural areas. Second, when the number of years of schooling, and the number of repeated years, are analysed, it is evident that many attend for less than four years. One example will suffice. A UNESCO study showed that half the children in urban primary schools in Guatemala in 1962 would complete six grades, while only 3·5 per cent would do so in rural areas. In Uruguay the comparable figures for completion of five grades were 73·6 per cent urban and 41·7 per cent rural. Figures of this order are still common, in spite of expansion in the last decade. The relative enrolments in secondary schools are lower still for rural children, and for girls. A recent estimate indicates that in poor rural areas less than one child in four, sometimes as few as one in ten or even less, attains a functional mastery of reading and writing; and this soon fades away if it is not kept in use, for which rural life gives little opportunity. The great majority of rural children who attend school gain no more than a transient smattering of general knowledge, which has little value except for the rare few who have a chance to continue at secondary school.

The unsuitability of existing formal schools for rural children has been commented on earlier. They divorce the children from their rural communities, ignore their culture, inculcate unsuitable attitudes related to urban life and fail to encourage an understanding of the environment in which they will grow up and live. As far as rural development is concerned they often do more harm than good. Sweeping as these generalisations are, they nevertheless apply in many situations. A small number of fortunate children gain, and

61

take advantage of schooling as a means of growing out of the limited background, and this opportunity should not be lost in the future, but most do not. These criticisms are widely made, and have much truth. The hopes that primary schools would equalise opportunities, and help social development, have proved to be false. It does not seem as if any amount of improvement of the curriculum or teaching methods could remedy the situation, for what is needed is a new form of education much closer to community life, and to its improvement.

The importance of non-formal education

Non-formal education denotes organised, systematic activities to provide learning in certain fields and for particular groups of children or adults. It is separate from formal schooling, and includes a variety of programmes to give adult literacy, occupational skills, agricultural extension and farmer training, community programmes in health, nutrition, family planning, cooperatives, etc. In organisation it is usually distinct from such institutions as schools, technical colleges etc.; although schools in some countries have a wide range of out-of-school activities, agricultural colleges often run extension programmes, and so on. There are basic differences in objectives, administration, finance, qualifications of teachers, provision of accommodation and facilities; but also areas of overlap, such as when some teachers are involved in both, and when there is dual use of accommodation. The extent and nature of non-formal education varies from one place to another: it may be predominantly a form of community development, or vocational education, or literacy and basic education, or merging into more recreational activities. It has developed irregularly over a long period of time, often growing from local initiatives, usually with little financial support. Its main purpose has been to supplement formal schooling in the advanced countries, and to provide some education for the very large proportion of the population for whom schools cannot be provided in the poorer developing countries, especially for the children and young persons in rural areas. Thus, it can be viewed on one hand as a movement towards 'lifelong education', and on the other as a vital factor in rural development.

Until recently there was no comprehensive survey of non-formal education in developing countries, but this has now been provided in a thorough and detailed report by the International Council for Educational Development, which has been made for the World Bank.[2] It shows how extensive and varied the activities have been, though its main focus was on non-formal programmes aimed at improving rural productivity and employment, and so on services for farmers, rural artisans, craftsmen and small entrepreneurs. In the course of preparatory studies twenty-five selected cases were examined in some detail; and agricultural education was much the largest part of the non-formal activities, mostly directed towards farmers, and with characteristically little provision for women. But there is also a bewildering assortment of unconnected activities, with great flexibility and diversity, free from administrative restrictions, such that hardly any developing country has attempted to survey the range of activities and relate them to the practical needs of development. There were three broad conclusions (p. 235):

> First, nonformal education – of the right kinds in the right places, properly tied to complementary efforts – is an indispensable and potent instrument of rural development.
>
> Second, even the poorest of countries – given a favorable political climate and determination by its leaders and people to build a better future – should be able to mobilize the resources and human energies for a considerable expansion of nonformal education in rural areas.
>
> Third, developing countries can forge ahead more quickly in non-formal education if given critical types of help from the outside. There is no shortage of ways for external agencies to assist strategically, but to do so with greatest effect they will be required to alter considerably their past policies, doctrines and models of operation.

In addition, three recurrent needs stood out as themes: for closer integration of non-formal programmes, more decentralisation, and greater equity. Non-formal education contributes little to development by itself, but is a necessary and often highly productive element of overall development programmes. The need for decentralisation arises from the great variations among rural areas, in resources, pattern of economic activities and potential, to which local programmes should be closely adapted. The need for greater equity is related to the basic difficulty in development that those who least need the help given by development programmes are those who most readily take advantage of them; while those who suffer most from poverty and ignorance are the least able to respond to the new opportunities. There is no easy solution to this problem, but it has to be kept in mind when devising programmes.

The most important general outcome of this study was its confirmation of the view that had been steadily gaining ground, to the effect that the kind of learning provided in formal schools is unsuited to transform rural societies. Its curriculum, values, incentives and rewards are oriented to a competitive urban society, and incompatible with the values and needs of rural development. What is wanted for the latter is an open-access, diversified and flexible rural-learning system. It must be cheap, easy to disseminate among isolated communities, and closely related to developmental projects: in brief, something that does not exist as yet.

World Bank programmes of aid

The largest source of aid for rural development is the World Bank. Their policy is set out in the Address to the Board of Governors by the President, Mr McNamara, on 30 September 1974.[1] He refers to the wide disparity of incomes in the developing countries, with roughly 40 per cent of the population in each country 'who are neither contributing significantly to their nation's economic growth nor sharing in its economic progress'. He then sets the focus of policy on the 'marginal' men and women, barely surviving in abject poverty on the margin of life, and comprising some 40 per cent, or 800 million, of the peoples of the developing countries. The emphasis was then placed 'not on the redistribution of income and wealth – as justified as that may be in many of our member countries – but rather on increasing the productivity of the poor, thereby providing for a more equitable sharing of the benefits of growth'. He then goes on to record five projects to illustrate how this policy is being put into effect:

> During the next five years our lending to agriculture should double, supporting projects whose total costs will approximate $15 billion and whose direct benefits should extend to 100 million rural poor.
>
> We expect the economic returns on these investments to exceed 15 per cent. They would be similar to the following five projects which were approved by the Bank's Board of Directors in a single two-week period this summer.
>
> 'A $10·7 million credit for agricultural development in the southern region of the Sudan which will provide a higher standard of nutrition for some 50,000 farm families through expanded food crops; will assist an additional 13,000 farm families through new cash crops; and will benefit roughly half the region's total population of three million people through improved, disease-free livestock.
>
> 'An $8 million credit for a comprehensive rural development project in Upper Volta, covering extension services, small-farmer credit, improved water resources, and greater access to health facilities; a project calculated, in all, to benefit some 360,000 individuals, 7 per cent of the country's cultivated land area.
>
> 'A $21·5 million credit for a broadly based livestock development program in Kenya, including provisions designed to assist traditional

nomadic herders; to improve 10 million acres of communal rangeland; and to expand wildlife areas in order to lessen the conflict for food and water between wildlife and cattle. The program will enhance the incomes of 140,000 rural inhabitants.

'An $8 million credit for an integrated rural development project in Mali providing farm inputs and equipment; an expanded functional literacy program; improved medical and veterinary facilities; and an agricultural research program. The program will reach over 100,000 farm families – some one million individuals – with agricultural services that are projected to triple their per capita incomes.

'A $30 million credit for a comprehensive dairy development project in India, providing for an increase in production of a million tons of milk a year, as well as for 100,000 heifers; and organizing small cattle owners into 1800 dairy cooperatives which will directly benefit some 450,000 farm families – $2\frac{1}{2}$ million individuals – the majority of whom own holdings less than two hectares in size, or are landless. The economic return of the project is estimated at more than 30 per cent on the capital invested.'

These are admirable projects, aimed directly at helping some of the poorest in each country, hesitant to infringe national sovereignty through becoming openly involved in questions affecting the redistribution of incomes. In the present economic and political climate, the plans are ambitious. To quote again from the report: 'Aid is a continuing social and moral responsibility, and its need now is greater than ever.' Yet there must be' serious doubts as to whether aid on this scale, and under the terms where loans are regarded as investment, can possibly suffice to meet the challenge. In the background are the international conferences referred to earlier; and certainly rural development has to be carried through the phase of increasing productivity to raise standards of living above bare subsistence, into the phase where social development can begin to stabilise population increase, and so ensure enough food and real improvements to the 'quality of living'. The terms of trade between the advanced countries and the Third World, and these issues, like those of moving towards more equitable societies, are essentially political.

Some rural development projects: Sudan, Ethiopia, India

An early example was the Gezira scheme in the Sudan, started under British colonial rule soon after the First World War as a major irrigation project to increase the production of cotton.[3] It was operated by a syndicate under government franchise which ensured control of economic and other objectives. Beginning with 100,000 acres, it expanded to about a million acres with 120,000 farm families. Its aim was economic improvement for these families; and with the help of close and continuous supervision, and of integrating good agricultural practice with effective marketing, under precise financial control, it clearly succeeded. The land was reapportioned to enable each family to have about thirty acres, land being rented at pre-development rates rather than expropriated, with tenants protected from eviction and prevented from making assignments. Financial control ensured the equitable distribution of profits, with a percentage set aside for social development. Economic growth came first, but programmes of social development were found to be necessary, as the farmers did not improve their conditions on their own. By 1940 there was political pressure to appoint Sudanese agricultural officers and administrators, and to involve selected farmers as extension agents, changes which were made after appropriate training without loss of productivity. The franchise of the syndicate was not renewed after 1950, and a revised scheme was brought in by an Act of 1960. It is a good example of an early project which achieved economic growth under a tightly managed system, with attention being given to social development in a second phase.

A recent example of a coordinated 'package' project is given by the Chilalo Agricultural Development Unit (CADU) inaugurated by the Swedish bilateral aid agency (SIDA) with the government of Ethiopia, initially for the period 1967–70.[4] The project covered an area of 650,000 hectares of arable land in the Chilalo region, with a population of 400,000 of whom 90 per cent lived in scattered homesteads along the one main road or on rough trails. Its aim was to bring about economic and social development by improving agriculture, especially for the poorer farmers; the few better off farmers were excluded, but could apply to participate. There were several main lines of development. First, improvement of crops and livestock, methods of crop growing and animal husbandry, zoning of areas for appropriate crops or animals, better implements and techniques, optimal use of fertilisers and pest control, etc. – in brief, a comprehensive approach to agricultural improvement, including training schemes. Second, the development of an effective trading system, including seeds, implements and equipment for home use, and the beginning of cooperatives. Third, development of the infrastructure, physical and administrative, and provision of credit. Fourth, efforts to improve health and nutrition, including supplies of clean water and more nutritious foods, and to improve the quality of life. A distinctive feature of the project is that CADU was set up as a separate unit within the Ethiopian Ministry of Agriculture, which exercised responsibility from the start, and shared in the costs. The project started with strong support by the Swedish specialists, but there was a firm programme for the training of Ethiopian counterparts and the handing over of duties to them. Near the end of the initial period, a joint Swedish–Ethiopian review group reported favourably; and a further agreement was signed to cover 1970–75, as a second phase of an overall thirteen year project, with one of the conditions prescribed by the Swedish government being for new tenancy legislation to be implemented in the project area within two years. An improvement in local administration was also required. The plan for 1970–75 provides for more extension education in agriculture, and an expansion of programmes of education for youth and adults, including women, especially in home economics. The project has owed much of its success to careful planning and coordination, and a question for the future is how it will fare when Swedish skills are withdrawn and it is incorporated into the general administration of the country.

India launched a massive Community Development Programme shortly after independence, expanding it to a national scale in the first Five-Year Development Plan.[5] This approach had grown slowly as a form of social welfare in British colonies in Africa, trying to encourage self-help in health, adult education and other aspects of community welfare; but when independence came these nations preferred to expand the provision of schools. It was a fresh approach in India, taking advantage of the long tradition of the movement for village development, and starting with a small scale project under the Ford Foundation. There is no space here to summarise so ambitious a scheme, of which there is a good short account in the ICED publication. In its early years there was a surge of enthusiasm, at a time when the excitement of political independence was still fresh. It stimulated local government by creating the panchayat structure, encouraging rural communities to participate, and enabling them to envisage the government as a source of help and not only a collector of taxes. Perhaps its greater impact was on the consciousness of the village peoples. But it could not overcome the tremendous obstacles in the way of improving the fearful poverty and near starvation endemic in rural India. In economic terms it was, inevitably, a failure: the requirements for economic growth were not there, and the population was rising inexorably, as it still is.

In two of these three examples the driving force came from an external advanced country; in the third it was to be self-help. The problem of what should be a fruitful combination between the former authoritarian approach, whether the source of authority is the government of the country or external, is a different issue; and the approach of stimulating initiatives for development within the rural communities themselves remains. It can be seen as one aspect of the political context of development, the importance of which is immediately apparent in a number of countries, of which Tanzania will be considered as an example.

Socialism and rural development in Tanzania

Among the newly independent nations of Africa, Tanzania has initiated the most carefully thought out and ambitious political transformation, under the exceptional leadership of President Nyerere.[6] His criticism of the deep division in African society between the governing élites – both the old colonial ones and those who have stepped into their shoes since independence – and the mass of rural peasants led him to formulate his ideas in 'Ujamaa: the Basis of African Socialism', a pamphlet which was published in 1962 a few months after independence; *ujamaa* being a Swahili word, derived from Arabic, meaning 'familyhood'. This was followed by 'Socialism and Rural Development' which described how 'the traditional African family lived according to the basic principles of ujamaa'; and how these were based in turn on three principles – respect for others in accordance with age, family relationships etc.; respect for shared property; and the obligation to work. And so the whole movement could be seen as the development of modern African socialism from the traditional African way of life, with little influence from China or Russia which had given much aid, or from other countries. He saw it as opposed equally to capitalism and doctrinaire socialism. Nyerere portrays a noble idealism: 'the objective of socialism in Tanzania (is) to build a society in which all members have equal rights and opportunities, in which all can live in peace with their neighbours without suffering or imposing justice, being exploited or exploiting, and in which all have a gradually increasing basic level of material welfare before any individual lives in luxury.' He saw this as flowing naturally from the African experience. 'The traditional African family lived according to the basic principles of ujamaa. . . . They lived together and worked together because this was how they understood life and how they reinforced each other against the difficulties they had to contend with. . . . The results of their efforts were divided unequally between them, but according to well-understood customs.' He acknowledged weaknesses in the African situation which should be remedied, especially poverty and the generally inferior position of women. His account of African tribal life with its innate socialism and democracy, from which his modern form of African socialism has it source, may seem to be somewhat idealised in the process, for the numerous tribes of Tanzania differ widely in the eyes of anthropologists: some show little sign of the three principles just quoted, in some cooperation may be confined to the family and in others to age-sets or labour teams, while many use hired labour and accumulate the ownership of land or cattle. Although many features of a simple, stable and supportive community are attractive, in general tribal life was short, often hard and sometimes cruel. Few educated Africans wish to revert to that kind of existence. However, when pride in the past helps to persuade isolated rural communities to improve their way of life and look ahead with idealism, it serves a valuable purpose.

In practice, early village settlement schemes proved to be expensive and ineffective, and a severe drought in 1965 added to economic difficulties. Nyerere's political party, the Tanzanian African National Union (TANU), had been made the sole party, but its reorganisation did not run smoothly, although it was eventually given a comprehensive framework organised in units of descending size covering all the people, the cells of ten houses being the smallest units, like the capillaries of the blood system, pervading the whole body politic. There was resistance in the countryside to the dislocation caused by forming Ujamaa villages; and the university students protested against having to do national service on the land in order to build the socialist state. This led to Nyerere reaffirming his philosophy in the Arusha Declaration of February 1967, which embodied his policies for Socialism and Self-Reliance and guidelines for TANU. It is a comprehensive statement that deserves to be read in full. It is more revolutionary in tone than his earlier pronouncements, calls for state ownership or control of all resources and production, aims at creating a fully socialist state, and makes no mention of Ujamaa villages.

A month later came 'Education for Self-Reliance', which set out to change the school system, eradicating the capitalist and competitive aspects, aiming at the inculcation of correct social attitudes and the production of good farmers in order to bring improvements in agriculture and village development. Primary schools were to prepare for the kind of life most children would lead, and not for selection for secondary education. The schools themselves were to be self-reliant communities, earning money to contribute to their expenses, with the children's work a part of their learning; and the same was to apply to colleges and other institutions. The schools with their reformed curricula are somewhat like the *écoles rurales* that have been tried elsewhere with little success. But they might have a better chance here as an integral part of a political transformation of society, if a really skilled approach could be adopted to teacher training, self instructional materials, etc., and this is being attempted.

Tanzania has few natural resources, and the population of fourteen million is thinly scattered over a large area, with poor communications.

Over 90 per cent are engaged in agriculture, mostly for subsistence, with some estates growing the sisal and some of the coffee, which, with cotton, form the main exports. Most of the peasants are not only illiterate, but very poor, struggling to grow enough food to support them on their small shambas. By any criteria, and quite apart from political considerations, agricultural development would present severe difficulties.

The programme to regroup all the countryside into Ujamaa villages lies at the heart of the planned transformation. Each village is notionally to have up to 3000 inhabitants, retaining rights to their own land, but developing as collective communities. The whole organisation of TANU was engaged in persuasion, and a large share of national resources was allocated in order to achieve rapid change. However, by 1973 only two million of the population, still a small minority, had been absorbed into the new collective villages, because of widespread resistance. Cattle owning tribes had too much to lose, and many others were reluctant to leave their traditional settlements in the bush, especially when this seemed to jeopardise the crops on which their food supply depended; although in poor agricultural areas the new villages offered fresh hope, and there was more progress. However, there was no controlled planning, and what could be regarded as constituting a ujamaa village was not clearly specified: as the movement was intended to be largely spontaneous, growing from the spirit of self-help, there was naturally a great variety. Some villages were aggregated by drawing together scattered peasants from a radius of five miles or so, which allowed continuity of crop cultivation. Others were old villages or settlement schemes reorganised. A few were constituted when peasants, usually from a single tribe, moved from one area to another. Given the variation in origin, agricultural potential, tribal composition etc., it is not surprising that villages range in size from 50 to over 5000 inhabitants. The loose form of organisation, and absence of statistics of crop production etc., make it difficult to evaluate progress; and this is a consequence of the view that the benefits should be social and moral, at least as much as material. But the difficulties and tensions have inevitably been very great.

Progress had been slow, and it seemed as though the persuasion and example on which Nyerere had relied, were insufficient. Eventually he declared in 1973 that all the rural population would have to be moved into Ujamaa villages by 1976, and TANU was given the task of doing this, backed by the army. Families were moved forcibly, some huts burned and shambas razed upon occasion; and within a year or so the figure of those re-settled had been increased to some five million, though it is difficult to know what significance can be attached to these figures put together under pressure. It is hard to say whether the remarkable enthusiasm, which had earlier been reported by observers from many parts of the country, will be tainted by the use of compulsion; or whether the high personal regard in which the President is still held, as well as the loyalty of TANU, will sustain the programme.

However, the economic situation has deteriorated seriously. Food production has declined sharply during two years of drought, and no doubt also as a consequence of millions of peasants being moved from their land – whatever the main reasons are, the government has become heavily dependent on foreign aid to import food and avoid starvation. The increase in oil prices has been an additional handicap, and the country is more or less bankrupt. Self-reliance is still the proclaimed objective, but dependence on aid is likely to continue for some years. The future of this idealistic experiment in creating a more egalitarian rural society, which could have great significance in Africa and beyond, appears to be in the balance. If it fails through lack of sufficient aid at a critical time, it will be a tragedy; for it is probably unique as an experiment by a non-communist state in developing without dependence on international aid and markets, while overcoming privilege in order to create a just and equitable society.

Kenya: development through economic growth

While Tanzania has sought to develop through a strongly socialist move towards a more egalitarian society, the approach in Kenya has been more open, aiming at fast economic growth to improve living conditions and provide more employment, encouraging aid from abroad and private enterprise, and helping local communities to take their own initiatives.[7] The government is less doctrinaire, seeking to foster 'self-help' by stimulating leadership from within communities – in this sense it could be described as more indigenous, and hence more African. Aiming at vigorous growth from what exists, policies can be more flexible to meet changing circumstances. The long period of stable government under Kenyatta since independence has attracted outside aid and investment, and there have been considerable advances in agriculture and industry, housing and communications. Nairobi has become a modern city, with considerable affluence and much poverty, and presenting a striking contrast to the rural areas. The problems are evident: population increasing faster than employment, leading to frustration and unrest; much of the new wealth going to a favoured minority, with development unevenly spread; and below the surface, tensions between the dominant Kikuyu and other tribes. The basic questions are how development can be stimulated and controlled, and abuses avoided. The stimulus was provided by Kenyatta with his stirring calls for 'harambee' in the early days

71

of independence which led to the building of local initiative freedom schools, and more recently to the so-called village polytechnics. This has helped to prepare the way for the current introduction of free primary education, not yet compulsory, but as a first stage free for all children in grades I to IV. The policy aims at providing free primary schooling for all children, with revised curricula, and increasing the output of teachers from training colleges; and for a time secondary expansion will be held back and few harambee secondary schools will be incorporated in the state system.

The formidable problems which Kenya faces in trying to give all children a basic primary education are characteristic of many Third World countries. The population of twelve million (in 1972) is increasing at about 3·5 per cent a year, and at that date 47·6 per cent were under the age of 14, while the literacy rate was about 40 per cent. In the first year when primary grades I to IV were made free, the enrolment rose from 450,000 to 1,100,000 in 1973–74 – a staggering increase for one year. The difficulty of financing this expansion is evident when the national income per head is estimated at K£46 and the recurrent costs are estimated (also for 1974–75) at K£26 per annum for primary, K£47·5 for secondary, K£198·6 for secondary technical, K£215·5 for primary teacher training, and K£1043·4 at the university. With a high birth rate and limited resources the cost cannot be met, except through outside aid. Moreover, the extent of full or partial unemployment, especially among the young, though a serious problem in many parts of the world, has reached an acute level in Kenya.

Kenya has thus embarked on an ambitious programme to provide full primary schooling without fees for all children, which will only be feasible with sustained foreign aid. This forms a major part of an overall development programme being financed by the World Bank and other agencies, and the aim is to achieve economic growth sufficient to raise the standard of living of all sections of the population; and incidentally to support the expanded educational system. Much depends on whether political stability can be maintained even when Kenyatta withdraws from active leadership, and whether the government will be able to sustain public support while taking difficult decisions needed to press ahead with development priorities. There is, however, another important question: namely whether an expansion of the existing system of primary and secondary schools can make a real contribution to rural as well as urban development; or whether it simply reinforces the imbalance between the two sectors, and exacerbates the dangerous increase of unemployment. It seems that what is wanted is some practicable alternative, and in the absence of this the policy is bound to continue.

China: a brief note

After the People's Republic of China was set up in 1949, the leaders under Mao Tse-tung struggled to reform the vast and varied country according to their own unfolding of communist ideals, closely in touch with Russia in the beginning, but otherwise isolated behind locked doors from the rest of the world for more than two decades. Recently, since the doors have been opened a little, it has been possible to do no more than begin to assess the difficulties, the nature of the remarkable transformation, and the continuing flux of leadership, policies and ideology. A good short account is given in a paper by Lee on 'Education and Rural Development in China Today',[8] and only a few brief comments will be made here.

During the first half of this century China was characterised by its enormous mass of peasants on the borderline of starvation, with high mortality from disease, and widespread illiteracy. Rural development lay at the centre of the revolutionary reforms – it still has a very high priority in the fourth development plan, for 1971–75. The drive for development has been on three main lines: literacy and mass education, agricultural and technical training, and improving health. Education has a different connotation from the usual cognitive and affective notions it carries in the West, for it is above all politically ideological, and after that essentially practical. It is a dual system, described in their phrase as 'walking on two legs', referring to formal schools and non-formal education. Just as education to revolutionise the thinking and attitudes of the mass of the people, especially rural peasants, is a first requirement in carrying through a revolution, so education now permeates every activity. It is ideological and practical at all levels, from nursery schools to universities. Broadly, a commune is responsible for middle schools, a production brigade for primary schools, and production teams for lower primary and non-formal education. As an outcome of the 'cultural revolution', the length of formal schooling was reduced from twelve years to nine, and the selection of students for more advanced education was to be done by communes after the young people had worked for at least three years on a farm or in a factory, the criteria for selection being more concerned with ideological correctness and zeal than abilities as a student. Selection is for the upper secondary to begin with, and then for vocational courses, few going to universities; and even in them theoretical studies alternate with practical work, and with periods as a productive worker in factory or farm – in order to avoid the emergence of free thinking scholars or an élite of well educated persons.

The main thrust in development, however, has been through the loose and all-pervading spread of non-formal education, with no set curriculum, strongly ideological, concerned with training to raise agricultural productivity, and springing up on local initiative wherever a need appears, in the village or in the fields or among a group of people; a spontaneous response to local needs, and lasting until they have been met. The stimulus is political and continual revivification of ideology through studying the thoughts of Chairman Mao – it is interesting to speculate how this basically rural and decentralised organisation differs from the present Russian system comprising a highly developed bueaucracy, maintained by a powerful secret police, carried over readily by the party from the hated secret police of the tsars. However that may be, and there appears to be a very extensive bureaucracy already in China, this infinitely flexible and directly practical plethora of non-formal education seems to have been a crucial influence in the development of agriculture, and also of public health. It is significant that China now seems confident about growing enough food for all its people without anxiety; and that the campaigns for improving standards of health, which have been very successful, have been accompanied by equally effective campaigns to reduce family size and stabilise the population. As far as can be judged, the achievement has no parallel outside China.

Reducing illiteracy has made relatively little progress, and it presents special difficulties. The very complex written form of the language is common throughout the country, although pronunciation of the characters varies beyond recognition among the numerous dialects. Efforts have been made to simplify the range of characters, for instance to a basic 500, or to transpose them into letters, either of which would simplify the situation; but then the language would no longer be common to all dialects, i.e. no longer a truly national language. An intractable problem.

One other feature of development in China deserves mention; and that is the way rural communes have gradually evolved some light industrial activities related to their agricultural needs. This has helped to minimise the sharp distinction between urban and rural levels of living and opportunities for employment, which often present difficulties in the Third World.

Cuba: communism near Latin America

The Cuban revolution of 1959 was achieved by guerrillas after years of fighting in the countryside, supported by the peasants, and it was natural that the revolutionary government should make great efforts to reduce illiteracy and give priority to rural development.[9] The campaign against illiteracy has received much attention for, unlike China, Cuba did not close its doors on the world. Its success was considerable, for the number counted as illiterate dropped by three-quarters during 1961–62, to less than a quarter of a million. Naturally, there have been difficulties in maintaining the level of literacy after the initial enthusiasm waned. A thorough reform of both formal schooling and non-formal education provided the vigorous thrust to change attitudes in support of the new communism, and education was pushed into every rural settlement. A fundamental reorganisation of the basis of agriculture was also essential, as sugar, the main product, is an estate crop requiring a large labour force at certain seasons, and only a small number for steady employment. The change involved setting up state farms, whose peak labour needs were met by drawing men temporarily from other jobs, thus overcoming the evils of the long established plantation system, clearly described by Beckford: 'On the whole the plantation has a demoralizing influence on the community. It destroys or discourages the institution of the family and so undermines the entire social fabric. It engenders an ethos of dependence and patronage and so deprives people of dignity, security and self-respect.'[10] It might be added that these comments do not apply to sugar plantations only; also that the 'social fabric' has never been very strong in the West Indies from the days of slavery onwards.

Land reform in two stages in 1959 and 1963 removed the root causes of rural inequality, and brought many unemployed labourers and large areas of inactive land into effective production. The drive for rural development also ensured that rural areas had at least an equal share with the towns of schools, hospitals and other services, and were fully involved in communal responsibilities, receiving preferential treatment in many ways.

Rural education was given priority in the effort to make primary schools available for all children, and an impressive number of new schools were built and provided with teachers. But the problems typical of undeveloped countries persist: the teaching is ineffective, and only a minority complete the six year course – and the pyramid narrows even more at secondary and higher levels. Whether the large investment in schooling does much to spread opportunities more equally or to raise productivity and improve living standards, remains in doubt, There are also large programmes of non-formal education, strongly ideological and with the aim of improving agricultural methods; and to take urban youth to study with rural youth in the countryside – not surprisingly, the two do not mix readily. On the whole, non-formal education seems to have had considerable impact in several directions; but the flexibility and lack of defined objectives make assessment difficult. There continue to be appeals from leaders for deeper changes in attitudes and approaches so that education can contribute more effectively to the social revolution.

The contribution of education to rural development

Until a decade or so ago the natural approach to reducing rural poverty was by improving agricultural productivity. Advanced countries had done this by developing agricultural institutes, extension services, cooperatives for better marketing etc., and this experience could be passed on to the Third World. But social attitudes there, and levels of education, and the whole complex infrastructure, were entirely different. The transfer had many difficulties, and it was gradually realised that rural development was the outcome of a complete network of interacting circumstances; and these varied from one locality to another according to soil, climate, rainfall, tribal customs and skills, laws on land tenure and inheritance, levels of education, government policies on taxes, etc. Thus development programmes have to be sensitively related to local circumstances, and their success depends largely on a coordinated approach – hence the weakness unless they are administered by one Minister with overall responsibility.

If peasant farmers are desperately poor, ignorant and unhealthy, then these circumstances have to be relieved before development can proceed further. But above a minimal level, attitudes and incentives become crucial; and it seems that even illiterate peasants often have a shrewd sense of whether a proposed change would have any advantages for them.[11] Incentives can be thought of in three general categories (1) rise in income (2) better living conditions (3) the spur of political ideology. If a new crop strain, agricultural technique or breed of farm animal is likely to bring a larger income, it will at least be given a trial. If better productivity leads to improved housing, water supply or other services, this will provide a stimulus, as in a communal village in China or Tanzania. Political ideology can also provide a strong incentive, up to a point, though farming had to be collectivised by force in Russia, and one peasant in Tanzania is said to have commented: 'You cannot feed on ujamaa'. However, there is also a need to qualify the notion of incentives by including a sense of equity. For instance, heavy sacrifices have been borne by Chinese peasants for many years since the revolution with typical courage and tenacity because all were sharing in the struggles. Similarly, a small farmer will give up half his income willingly to his communal village, but not if it has to go to a landlord. Again, farmers are encouraged to increase production if the rural areas are really getting a full share of government finances – which would be unusual.

There has been a tendency to underestimate the influence of political aspects of government, as opposed to administrative aspects, which is understandable as long as international convention forbids any interference with a nation's sovereignty, or more specifically with its internal policies (but see the earlier comment on the renewal of the CADU contract). The borderline is delicate in relation to aid between trying to encourage policies, e.g. on land tenure or population control, which seem to be needed for a development project, and seeming to intervene in internal policies in a neo-colonialist manner.

The literature on development includes the 'transformationist' views of those who think progress in many Third World countries can only be attained through revolutionary changes, and the 'gradualists' who see progress as the cumulative outcome of many developmental projects. To the latter should be added the emphasis on rapid economic growth, which is the main attraction of the free market, heavy investment approach. To discuss these questions is far beyond the scope of this book; and the point which is being stressed here is that the revolutionary changes in China, Cuba and Tanzania, which have been referred to briefly, have certainly given rise to powerful motivation for development – whatever their other consequences may be. Whether, or how much, political ideologies of this kind will spread in Asia, and perhaps also in Africa and Latin America, is largely a matter of conjecture. What we are concerned with is the need for incentives in order to encourage rural development, and political ideology can provide one form of incentive; but there are other, more immediate ones, if a government is determined enough to provide them.

There is no clearly defined minimum of schooling essential to provide a base for development in all the variety of rural situations, either in terms of the number of years of schooling or of the proportion of children attending school. In general it is an advantage if a fair proportion become literate, preferably not fewer than a third or a half; but this is an oversimplified guideline.

A study of experience gained in a variety of development projects suggests that the contribution of education can be envisaged as serving several functions:

1   To give sufficient literacy and a basic education, to enable young people to read pamphlets, local news sheets, etc., consider evidence, and decide what to do in practical situations in their lives.

2   To provide a continuing flow of information in practical learning situations, especially for youth and adults, covering better methods in agriculture, nutrition, health, literacy and many aspects of community development.

3   To provide 'modern learning systems' for those eager to carry their studies further in general education or pre-vocational subjects, in preparation for attending secondary schools or vocational institutes. This would require students to have sufficient attainment in basic

education to enable them to take advantage of learning packages in rural isolation without specialist teachers.

4 All these aspects would be permeated by political ideology in communist countries, from the earliest pre-school education up to, and including, university studies. In more democratic countries, much less attention is usually given to political education, a situation inherited from the Western tradition.

) Most developing countries do not have the resources to give all children a full primary school course; and in schools where teaching has to contend with many difficulties it seems that a satisfactory basic education required about six years. The curriculum should be related to local conditions, but it is not feasible to provide wholly distinct rural and urban curricula. If the curriculum is kept simple, the schools should provide for as many children as possible.

Non-formal education, covering the full range of extension education and community development, makes a direct and flexible contribution to development. It is not an alternative to basic schooling, which gives a necessary foundation for the subsequent effective use of 'learning packages' etc.[12] Usually it draws on all those in a community with suitable knowledge or skills, is not institutionally organised, and does not depend on trained teachers. In many countries the head of a village school is also expected to be a leader in community development. This provides a focus for developing non-formal activities, although it often leads to a conflict of interests, when a teacher will usually follow instructions from his administrative superior, rather than the interests of the village, for he is part of the formal bureaucracy. A teacher can only be truly involved in rural community education if the system is decentralised to such an extent that he becomes part of the community, and responsible to it and not to an administrative bureaucracy under the central government (unless there is a complete change of outlook in the central ministry).

The third function outlined above is the least developed. It envisages the use of simple and cheap modern technology to provide 'distance learning packages' as part of what has been described as a 'comprehensive, flexible and diversified open-access rural learning system'.[13] Rather a mouthful; but it incorporates two ideas – that opportunities should be available to all with satisfactory basic schooling who would be prepared to make sufficient effort on their own initiative; and that admission to secondary schools as boarders would be made on this basis, and not on examinations at the end of the primary course – thus leaving the primary school free to become cooperative in its teaching instead of individually competitive as at present. In effect, selection for secondary schooling would depend on sustained voluntary study and the ability to take advantage of learning packages without specialist teachers.

The fourth function speaks for itself; but it raises the serious question whether education in democratic countries should not also be more politically conscious, at least involving democratic approaches to class learning and school organisation, in accordance with the cultural traditions of the locality. The teaching of 'civics' etc. has little influence. What is wanted is a fresh attitude to relationships in a school, replacing the authoritarian attitude of the teachers, giving children democratic responsibilities, and encouraging cooperation among them, in learning as well as in other activities. This change could happen once competitive selection for secondary education can be eliminated when the educational system has been transformed to serve the functions indicated.

Clearly these functions do no more than give a set of guidelines which could be adapted to a variety of conditions. They do not constitute a 'model', and the theoretical understanding of the complex flux of interactions involved in development is still much too inadequate for that. But this does represent a more comprehensive and flexible approach than has been generally envisaged as yet. In particular, it seeks to replace the single ladder of primary and secondary schools by a more flexible system comprising several different components which would supplement one another, and of which the basic school – and later, usually after an interval, the secondary school – would form a part.

Underlying the whole notion of rural development is that it should improve 'qualities of living'. This should be viewed in a fresh perspective following the international conferences of 1974, especially those on population and food. The importance of being self-supporting in food is clear to every government because of its direct impact on foreign exchange for imports. The impact of population increase is less direct. But, as in China, there can be no doubt of the value of a strong policy to control population, limiting its increase to what the national economy, resources of land, etc., can support. To have extensive health education without equally extensive population education (and related provision of facilities) is, to say the least, myopic. This would have to form part of the overall programme of rural development – equally important as raising agricultural productivity.

Notes

[1] Address to the Board of Governors by R. S. McNamara, President of the

World Bank Group, 30 September 1974; and *Rural Development: Sector Policy Paper*, Washington DC, 1975.

² P. H. Coombs and Manzoor Ahmed, *Attacking Rural Poverty: How Non-Formal Education can Help*, Johns Hopkins University Press, Baltimore, 1974. See also the parallel report by P. H. Coombs, R. C. Prosser and Manzoor Ahmed, *New Paths to Learning for Rural Children and Youth*, International Council for Educational Development, Essex, Connecticut, 1973.

³ A. Gaitskell, *Gezira: a Story of Development in the Sudan*, Faber and Faber, London, 1959.

⁴ B. Nekby, *CADU: an Ethiopian Experiment in Developing Peasant Farming*, Prisma, Stockholm, 1971.

⁵ G. Hunter, *The Administration of Agricultural Development – Lessons from India*, Oxford University Press, London, 1970.

⁶ The following provide an introduction:
J. K. Nyerere, *The Arusha Declaration*, 1967, and *Socialism and Rural Development*, 1968, Government Printer, Dar es Salaam.
J. King, *The Planning of Non-Formal Education in Tanzania*, International Institute for Educational Planning, Paris, 1967.
J. Connell, *The Evolution of Tanzanian Rural Development*, Institute of Development Studies, Sussex University, Brighton, Communication Series no. 110, 1973.

⁷ J. R. Sheffield, *Education in Kenya: an Historical Study*, Teachers College Press, New York, 1973.

⁸ H. P. Lee, 'Education and Rural Development in China To-Day' in the *World Year Book of Education 1974*, pp. 209–33, Evans, London, 1974.

⁹ R. R. Fagen, *The Transformation of Political Culture in Cuba*, Stanford University Press, Stanford, 1969.

¹⁰ G. L. Beckford, *Persistent Poverty: Underdevelopment in Plantation Economies of the Third World*, Oxford University Press, New York, 1972.

¹¹ A very useful survey is given in P. Foster and T. R. Sheffield (eds), 'Education and Rural Development', in the *World Year Book of Education, 1974*, Evans, London, 1974.

¹² See the references in note 2, and also:
T. R. Sheffield and V. P. Diejomaoh, *Non-Formal Education in African Development*, African American Institute, New York, 1972.

¹³ See the first reference in note 2, p. 253.

The following references may also be of interest:

D. Brokensha and P. Hodge, *Community Development: an Interpretation*, Chandler, San Francisco, 1969.

T. R. Batten, *Communities and their Development*, Oxford University Press, London, 1957.

A. F. Raper, *Rural Development in Action – The Comprehensive Experiment at Comilla, East Pakistan*, Cornell University Press, Ithaca, 1970.

T. Dejene and S. E. Smith, *Experiences in Rural Development* (bibliography for Africa), American Council on Education, Washington, 1973.

A. H. Bunting (ed.), *Change in Agriculture*, Praeger, New York, 1970.

T. Malassis, *Développement Economique et Programmation de l'Education Rurale*, UNESCO, Paris, 1966.

P. J. Foster and A. R. Zollberg (eds), *Ghana and the Ivory Coast: Perspectives in Modernization*, Chicago University Press, Chicago, 1971.

R. Jolly (ed.), *Education in Africa: Research and Action*, East Africa Publishing House, Nairobi, 1969.

6   Education and the Modern Urban Sector

The appeal of the city

The growth of cities in many developing countries in the last three decades has been far more rapid than occurred in any of the advanced countries when they were becoming industrialised. The process of industrialisation in the latter was in general more closely related to new industrial techniques than to the extent and level of education – Britain's education was less developed than that of continental Europe in the latter part of the nineteenth century, yet Britain was industrialising more rapidly. Moreover, industrialisation was accomplished at a time of low population growth, with urban expansion barely keeping pace with the growth of industry; and, although working conditions were deplorable, unemployment was low, and cyclical rather than structural. The improvement of sea transport, and the opening of the Suez canal, brought new markets for industrial products within easy reach; and it was an era of expanding trade.

The contrast with the present conditions in which urbanisation is taking place in developing countries is apparent. They have to compete for markets for their industrial products with countries that are technologically far more advanced, and their only advantage lies in labour-intensive industries, apart from the local processing of agricultural products. Much has been written about the scope for 'intermediate technology', which often involves the local production of equipment of simplified design, which could be made more cheaply than the imported equivalent, and which would serve its purpose sufficiently well.[1] This is certainly a valuable line of development; but its application is much too limited to provide a general basis for industrialisation in developing countries – for technology is advancing continually, and an attempt to remain substantially at the level of hand tool technology in the age of computers would offer scant hope for the future.

As we have seen already, the main hope for the future of the Third World lies in rural development: the evidence in support of this view is overwhelming. Many countries will be unable to feed their expanding populations unless they have a strong policy for rural development, even if their foreign exchange is spent on buying food instead of promoting development.

There will also be industrial development, but in most countries without oil it will be on a relatively small scale. This does not correspond at all with what both the leaders and the mass of the people want in almost all developing countries, for it is the modern urban sector that has a magnetic appeal. No doubt this is quite irrational, but aspirations often are; and there are many pressures in support of their views. Quite apart from industrialisation, effective development programmes require modern forms of government planning and administration, with a civil service which is inflated by European standards, as well as all the apparatus of politics, whether 'democratic' or 'one-party' or under military control. The operations of the network of UN and other agencies, and the increase in international trade, help to swell the visible tide of modernisation; prestige hotels and large office blocks become the proud symbols of progress – on the surface.

Urban 'growth' or 'explosion'?

Already there is serious urban unemployment in developing countries, as the population of working age has increased, during the last three decades especially, much faster than the demand for workers. The growth in population has had two main causes: a high rate of increase of the urban population, and extensive migration from the countryside – and both of these have implications for education. The consequence has been a rate of urban expansion far ahead of industrial development.[2]

Such data as exist indicate that the developing countries have higher birth rates and lower mortality rates in urban areas than in rural ones. The differences are not large, and may be due to the easier spread of preventive medicine in towns than countryside. The result is that the rate of population increase is even higher in urban than rural areas – in striking contrast to the situation when industry was developing in Western Europe. At that time, poor hygiene and nutrition in the towns, and very unhealthy working conditions in factories, gave a lower rate of population growth than in the countryside. However, the high natural rate of increase of urban population is no more than a part of the story, as we have seen, for there has also been a continuing flow of immigrants into the towns. It has been estimated that the urban population of developing countries increased during the decade 1950–60 by about 60 per cent, of which nearly a half was natural growth and just over a half was rural–urban immigrants, the total increase approaching 100 million. During the following decade, 1960–70, the total increase was some 130 million, of which rural–urban immigration accounted for just under a half.[3] One of the implications of this situation for education is the impossibility of planning to have two different systems, with different urban and rural curricula, when there is so much migration between them. In practice movement to and fro is much more frequent than the net figures indicate, for there is a constant flow of individuals from peasant families visiting a town for some months, often staying with a member of the extended family or the same tribe; and likewise workers from the town going on visits to the countryside, often buying a piece of land or a house with their savings. This continual flux of movements in addition to immigration prevents a sharp separation between towns and countryside.

Estimates of urban expansion for the half century from 1950 to 2000, a period already half in the past, indicate that it will rise in the advanced countries from 500 million to 1,000 million (with 100 million of the increase being by migration from the countryside, where the population would continue to decline). The equivalent expansion in the developing countries during the same period will be from 500 million to 2,200 million, in addition to which the rural population will double from 1,400 million to an estimated 2,800 million. It is a very alarming prospect. By the turn of the century half of the world's population is likely to be living in cities; and the urban slums and shanty towns of the Third World will double within the next ten years. That is why measures to stabilise populations are desperately urgent, even though they would take some time to have much effect. At best, if the rates of population increase were to decline soon in Asia, Latin America and Africa, enormous efforts would still be needed to improve conditions and reduce unemployment in urban slums – otherwise there will be growing frustration, desperation and violence.

Two suggestions have been made to alleviate conditions in the large urban slums. The first gives priority to 'minimum cost' programmes of improvement; and this is supported by the World Bank. The second is to encourage the great variety of indigenous 'self-help' efforts, many of them local, yet drawing on small initiatives which can bring a cumulative improvement in community feeling as much as in physical conditions. For instance, instead of the government striving to clear shanty towns and illegal squatters with bulldozers (at great cost, even when alternative housing is not built), the occupants could be encouraged to carry out their own improvements, with a little government help, such as the provision of simple tools – not enough to make them dependent on government support instead of doing things themselves. These two approaches are woefully short of beginning to solve the fundamental problems on a world scale, but at least they are doing something now: a worthwhile palliative, though they will do little to relieve the fearful shanty towns of Calcutta (which is said to have at least one and a half million unemployed), Bangkok, Manila, Djakarta, Buenos Aires, Lagos, etc.

The situation is bound to raise questions for education. What form of education would be appropriate for children in these slums, how can it be provided, and should it contribute to improving the conditions? Also, does the kind of education provided for rural children encourage them to migrate to towns and cities, as is often claimed, by giving them 'urban attitudes'?

Problems of rural–urban migration

The usual explanation is in terms of the interaction between 'push' influences from the rural environment and 'pull' influences from the urban environment. These influences vary from one situation to another, but how they operate in a particular set of conditions is bound to be largely a matter of conjecture, especially as data are sporadic. However, the factors commonly regarded as significant can be summarised as follows:

1   The 'push' effect of high rural population density in relation to the land resources, which presses many people, younger members of large families in particular, to leave the countryside in search of better opportunities in towns or cities.

2   The much higher apparent urban incomes exert a strong 'pull' effect. The income differential between an unskilled worker and an agricultural labourer in Western countries during the nineteenth century was slight, ranging perhaps from nothing to some 30 per cent. In developing countries urban incomes are much higher than agricultural ones, and estimates indicate that the differences vary between 100 per cent and 200 per cent or more. Hence the 'pull' is much stronger than when the present advanced countries were industrialising, even though it may be partly offset by the high urban unemployment.

3   Evidence shows that the more years of schooling rural children have, the more they wish to migrate to a city. There is a widespread belief that this is partly because the curriculum and the outlook of teachers are 'urban biased', though it is an impression which cannot be quantified. Nonetheless, it seems probable that the increase in rural primary schooling has contributed to the migration. Moreover, rural school attendance is generally much lower than in cities, and so this factor is likely to have a growing influence as it increases in the future.

4   The appeal of city life, mentioned earlier in this chapter, has a strong 'pull' effect: the city offers 'modern life' and escape from the restrictions of traditional rural communities, as well as the chance of higher earnings.

The relative importance of these factors, and of others such as social, political, religious and tribal influences, vary from one country, region or locality to another; and they are not susceptible, at any rate as yet, to being expressed in the form of a simple model. Even so, any change in educational provision which reduced the 'push' effect on migration would deserve support.

Problems of high urban unemployment

There is no doubt that urban unemployment is a very serious problem in the Third World, growing larger in total as cities go on expanding rapidly. Precise data are not available, because of difficulties over definitions as well as incomplete statistics. Unemployment in industrial countries can be recorded easily because a job comprises a regular working week, on an agreed basis of pay, carried on through the year; and unemployed persons usually register for weekly social welfare payments. In a preindustrial rural community, however, the whole notion of set hours of daily work throughout the year is altogether alien: work depends on the rhythm of seasons, the incidence of rainfall etc., and consists of tasks to be completed. A considerable proportion of the inflated population of Third World cities has carried over the rural attitudes brought with migration from the countryside. Few persons get regular work in industry, and many are employed in simple production of goods, doing minor repairs and odd jobs in the 'informal' sector. As a general guide, it seems that unemployment and underemployment together amount to about 25 per cent of the potential working population in many Third World countries. More specific figures for open unemployment in urban areas include the following: Sri Lanka 15·0 per cent, Kenya 14·9 per cent, Colombia 13·6 per cent, Philippines and Ghana 11·6 per cent.[4] More recent figures would probably be higher, in several instances rising to as much as 20 per cent, following the trends in both developing and advanced countries; and it is surprising that these figures of 10 per cent and over of open unemployment (to which there should often be added a similar extent of underemployment) are accompanied by high economic growth rates in many of these countries.

The situation had become so serious that emphasis was given to increasing employment when ILO launched its World Employment Programme in 1969 as a contribution to the UN's Second Development Decade. As part of the overall approach, comprehensive employment strategy missions were sent to Colombia, Iran, Kenya and Ceylon (before it was renamed Sri Lanka).[5] The first of the mission reports, on Colombia, changed the focus of policy from being to create more jobs, to being essentially a problem of overcoming poverty: there were enough work opportunities, but earnings were too low for a reasonable standard of living. Thus, the problems of unemployment had merged with those of poverty; hardly surprising in view of the difficulties, already mentioned, of defining unemployment in the Third World. As it happens, the measurement of earnings avoids the awkward question of the extent to which people are regarded as underemployed if they would like to work more to increase their income, if they could find suitable opportunities, for that would involve measuring desires and attitudes. The emphasis given to poverty led to examining ways in which the benefits of economic growth could be more equitably distributed, in addition to means for increasing employment.

The report on Kenya set a new approach in recognising the extent of small enterprises, employing fewer than ten people to make goods for the poor on a labour intensive basis, and the significance of this sector of the economy.

When considering the relationship between education and unemployment, it is necessary to distinguish two levels of imbalance. The overall imbalance between labour supply and demand is the root cause of unemployment; and the nature and extent of education has little direct effect on this relationship, as it cannot make new jobs (apart from employing more people as teachers). But education has a strong impact on the structural imbalance included within total employment; that is, on the failure to match educational expectations with job opportunities. This comes out clearly in the Colombia, Ceylon and Kenya reports.

It therefore becomes important to analyse the overall unemployment into separate categories, of which the most important are:

1   Visible and invisible unemployment, and underemployment.
2   Unemployment among those leaving (a) primary schools, (b) secondary schools, and (c) universities.
3   Youth unemployment, as an age group.
4   Underemployment with earnings below a minimum subsistence level.

Our concern here will be with youth unemployment in relation to levels of education.

Unemployment of the educated

In general, unemployment among those leaving school is higher than among adults, sometimes much higher in numbers and as a percentage. The young form a high proportion of the rapidly expanding populations of most developing countries: it is common for 40 per cent of the population to be

88

under fifteen years old, and 60 per cent under the age of twenty. Therefore the labour market is saturated with the young, most of whom in cities are school leavers; and it would have to be very efficient to absorb them all quickly even if there were enough vacancies. An important index is therefore, as in advanced countries, the average duration of unemployment in each category. The problem of youth unemployment, largely in the search for a first job, can often be seen as another aspect of educated unemployment. Thus Blaug refers to the situation in the Philippines in 1965 when the general rate of unemployment was 8 per cent, but for primary leavers it was 55 per cent, those leaving high school 26 per cent and college graduates 13 per cent; and at the same time half of all the unemployed were below the age of twenty-five and still looking for their first job.[6] Apart from other considerations, the extent to which a country's educational system has been developed – which varies between wide extremes, as we have seen in an earlier chapter – is likely to affect the issue.

However, despite all the complexities and the many unresolved questions awaiting further research, there is a considerable body of evidence indicating a widespread mismatch between jobs in the labour market and the expectations generated by the educational system. This emerges clearly in the Ceylon report, where the main problem is unemployed secondary school leavers; and also in the Kenya report, where primary school leavers are the largest group of unemployed. It would not help, in the view of the missions, to apply a quota to schools or to make more jobs, while leaving the structure of wages etc. unchanged. 'The root of the problem lies in the interaction of the conventional education system and the wage and salary structure through the allocation of jobs and wages by reference primarily to educational qualifications.'[7] The overall relationship between the development of education and economic growth seems to be long term, and rather diffuse in being concerned with attitudes and readiness to initiate as much as with skills; but it is possible to think more precisely of educational reforms that would affect the unemployment of the educated young. Here the discussion is in general terms, and does not take account of deep rooted historical causes operating in situations such as the unemployment of graduates in India.[8]

Some implications for education

In the search for possible solutions, it is necessary to keep in mind the conclusion reached earlier, that education can have relatively little influence on development except as part of an integrated policy. For example, if school curricula were to be reformed with a view to reducing the rural–

urban migration, this would have little effect unless the excessive disparity between rural and urban incomes was substantially reduced. Similarly, an improvement of the mismatch between education and jobs requires a reform of wage and salary structure as much as of the educational system.

The first question to be asked in any given situation is whether the lack of balance is mainly due to an overproduction of highly educated persons, as might be considered to be the case, for example, in India. The direct response would notionally be to reduce the output; but such an over-simplified approach would be politically and socially difficult, and likely to cause new complications unless it were part of a fresh policy: simply to reduce educational opportunities would hardly gain much support in a democracy. Moreover, in most developing countries there is already a fine sieve of examinations between primary and secondary schools, and another for admission to universities. The sieve can be made finer still by increasing fees or other costs, especially at college and university level, but this is socially unattractive.

Another approach is to enforce an interval at one or two places as the child progresses up the educational ladder, of which in most developing countries each rung is mounted on successfully completing an end-of-year examination. In the case of failure, the year is repeated. In the event of cumulative discouragement, then one more pupil steps off the ladder to add to the toll of dropouts. Certainly an enforced interval will reduce the output of better educated young people, with the likelihood that those with good support from their families will find it easier to persist. This approach is being tried in some countries, notably in China, as we have seen, where selection of those to continue their education is largely on political criteria. In more democratic countries, an enforced barrier preventing all students, including keen ones, from going on studying would seem to have a number of disadvantages, at least unless it could be combined with some other forms of opportunity.

Another line of approach is to make curricula more appropriate, bringing in prevocational studies. In varying degrees this is happening in most countries, but with too few resources, and it is inherently a long term process. Moreover, it leads to major tasks in the retraining of teachers, and new forms of initial training. The local or regional revision of curricula also has to be conducted within limits because many children migrate between country and city.

A radical proposal in the Ceylon report is that examinations should be abolished, their place being taken by aptitude tests. The purpose would be to force teachers to step out of the regimentation of didactic teaching and repeated examining, encouraging them to interest and involve their pupils, giving more scope to keen and lively teachers, and diminishing the whole competitive atmosphere which schools at present impose on children. It would not happen easily, and teachers would have to be extensively re-trained. Parents and older children would oppose what they would see as a withdrawal of opportunities. Examinations would be set up for admission to higher study and attractive jobs. Perhaps most important of all, suitable aptitude tests do not exist, and could not be quickly developed.

The strong plea for the more or less complete abolition of school examinations is so much a feature of the reports that it is worth quoting what the Joint Chiefs of the Kenya mission say about it.[9]

> In Kenya, as in so many other countries, the school examination system has increasingly become the dominant device for deciding who will go on to secondary and higher education and who, in turn, will get the good jobs. Given the very rapid rate of educational expansion when compared with the rate of growth of well-paid jobs, the task of selection has year by year become more burdensome and the backwash effect on the earlier stages of education has grown ever more disastrous. Increasing numbers of children leave school labelled as rejects or failures, so that the psychological tension to which students are subjected at examination time is extremely severe; even those who succeed do so to an increasing extent by learning to qualify rather than by learning to understand or by developing the initiative and inner resourcefulness which would be useful to them in tackling any one of a thousand practical problems in their locality, their homes, or their farms. The pernicious effects of examinations are not confined to a few weeks a year – being the dominant influence, they interfere with and destroy the whole pattern of what is learnt throughout the year.
>
> The mission felt that nothing less than a radical change in the entire examination system would be adequate. First, the extreme inequalities between districts and between good and bad schools would have to be tackled by introducing a basic quota under which a certain proportion of primary school leavers from every school would be given secondary school places. (Detailed statistical analysis of past examination results showed that the examination as a selection device had virtually no predictive validity.) Second, a number of bonus quotas could be made available for the schools within each district whose over-all examination results were well above average – thus providing school-focused incentives to spur teachers, parents and students to raise the quality of schools. Third, the examination itself would have to be changed, so as to improve its content and reliability and to supplement the 'book

learning' parts with tests designed to assess grasp of local problems, as well as ability to deal with them.

In a similar vein the Ceylon and Kenya reports propose that students on completion of their secondary school courses should have to work or do community service for two or three years before applying to a university; and that universities should select for admission on the basis of reports on their work or community service, reports from their teachers, and aptitude tests, with credit given for part-time courses taken during the interval. It is suggested that this would discourage the less keen students, and would improve motivation for study. There would inevitably be difficulties in making any such change, including the problem of evaluating reports from very disparate sources. But on balance this proposal has the advantage that, if adopted, it should improve the match between aspirations and opportunities, and might also reduce the demand for higher education.

The problem of making recommendations that may be politically feasible underlies the reports, as shown in the following comments:[10]

One important conclusion to emerge from the structural approach is that aggregative analyses of employment problems were in many countries not very meaningful: it is often more helpful to analyse incomes, work frustration and labour utilisation, sector by sector and district by district. Moreover, one cannot be concerned only with what people in the labour force do, or even with the activities of the adult population. The direction in which the missions have clearly been leading is towards concern with the patterns of all human activities, through different stages of people's lives. The focus of concern is thus shifted from economic activities (from 'unemployment' or even 'employment' problems) to concern with all forms of economic and social deprivation, and the role of employment strategy in their cure.

Another dimension which has been opened up has been awareness of the political dimensions of problems. As will be shown shortly, implementation of all three reports has been very partial, at best. This raises questions such as what weight a government actually gives to employment objectives, what freedom of manoeuvre it possesses given its relationships to key interest groups, both domestic and foreign, what costs would be involved in adopting an employment-oriented strategy, and how those who would benefit from such a policy could be made vocal and more powerful.

Non-formal education may be as important in urban areas as in the countryside, on the lines suggested in the preceding chapter. Literacy campaigns also have a part, but neither are sufficient for those children who have no formal schooling, however important they may be in supplementing it.

Clearly there is no simple solution. The problem of unemployment of youth, including those with various levels of education, is serious enough to make it imperative to search for remedies. After considering one or two case studies in modernisation in the next chapter, we shall turn our attention again to the problems of unemployment in relation to education and development.

Notes

[1] A simple introduction is given by E. F. Schumacher, *Small is Beautiful*, Blond and Briggs, London, 1973.

[2] P. Bairoch, *Urban Unemployment in Developing Countries*, ILO, Geneva, 1973.

[3] Bairoch, op. cit., p. 43.

[4] D. Turnham, *The Employment Problem in Less Developed Countries: A Review of Evidence*, OECD Development Centre, Paris, 1971.

[5] The general strategy is given in the first reference, and the reports of the four missions in the succeeding references, all being published by the ILO, Geneva:

ILO: Scope, approach and content of research-oriented activities of the World Employment Programme, 1972

Towards full employment: a programme for Colombia, 1970.

Matching employment opportunities and expectations: a programme of action for Ceylon, 2 vols, 1971.

Employment, incomes and equality: a strategy for increasing productive employment in Kenya, 1972.

Employment and incomes policy for Iran, 1972.

[6] This reference gives a valuable analysis of the problems involved in the relationship between education and unemployment:

M. Blaug, *Education and the Employment Problem in Developing Countries*, ILO, Geneva, 1973.

[7] Kenya report, see note 5, pp. 10–11.

[8] M. Blaug, R. Layall and M. Woodhall, *The Causes of Graduate Unemployment in India*, Allen Lane, London, 1969.

[9] H. Singer and R. Jolly, 'Unemployment in an African Setting: Lessons of the Employment Strategy Mission to Kenya', *International Labour Review*, vol. 107, no. 2, February 1973.

[10] R. Jolly, D. Seers and H. Singer, 'The Pilot Missions under the World Employment Programme', in *Strategies for Employment Promotion*, ILO Employment Research Papers, Geneva, 1973.

The following references are also likely to be of interest:

K. Little, *West African Urbanization*, Cambridge University Press, Cambridge, 1965.

B. Ahamed and M. Blaug (eds), *The practice of manpower forecasting: a collection of case studies*, Elsevier, Amsterdam, 1973.

D. J. Dwyer (ed.), *The City in the Third World*, Macmillan, 1974.

7   Nigeria as an Example of the Problems of Modernisation

Problems of rural–urban education

Some of the problems of development in rural and urban conditions have been considered in the last two chapters. In Chapter 5 the reasons were set out for believing that the kind of formal schooling found in most developing countries is ill suited or even harmful for rural development; and suggestions were made of four main functions which should be served by education in rural areas. Chapter 6 paid attention to the serious extent of unemployment in the Third World, especially of youth, and measures which have been proposed to improve the situation; and one of the important series of inter-related measures is a far-reaching transformation of the educational system. The problem of unemployment, and especially of poverty arising from sporadic, partial employment with low earnings, affects rural and urban areas alike; though its impact on individuals can be ameliorated to some extent in rural communities where personal relationships are closer, and which usually grow most of their own food. What emerges clearly from the discussion is that radical changes seem to be required in the system of education, and they should apply to both the rural and urban situations – for there is movement between the two in both directions, although the net result is usually a large migration from the countryside to towns and cities. However, it is evident from the difficulties in getting acceptance for measures to reduce unemployment that political considerations, as well as the complex of local circumstances, are important. This chapter considers how the development of education in a particular country – and Nigeria is chosen as an example – is affected by the interplay of political, historical, social and other factors.

Nigeria: a country of diversity

Nigeria is the largest nation of Africa, with a population approaching eighty million, and provides a good case study because of its cultural diversity, its contrasting rural and urban environments, and its determination to modernise rapidly by using its oil income.[1]

The country has an area of 350,000 square miles, more than three times the size of Britain, and is divided into three climatic zones: a belt of tropical rain forest a hundred miles wide along the coast, hot and very humid; a broad middle area of savannah grassland, warm and with good rainfall; and in the north a large area, hot and dry, with sparse vegetation which merges with the Sahara desert along the border with the state of Niger. The southern half of the country is fed by the river Niger and by its tributary the Benue, which form the west and east limbs of a large Y in the middle of the country. The population is negroid, with seven main ethnic groups: Yoruba, Hausa, Fulani, Ibo, Kanuri, Tiv and Ibibio providing four-fifths of the total, the remainder being made up of many smaller ethnic groups. There is a corresponding variety of languages, perhaps some 400, though about half of the population speak Hausa, Yoruba or Igbo as a first or second language; and there are national radio broadcasts in nine languages, as well as English, which forms the common language (there is no 'official' language).

The history of present day Nigeria is derived from two series of empires, one in the savannahs and the north, the other in the coastal forest areas in the south. The former include the Ghana empire which spread from the Atlantic to the Sahara between the sixth and thirteenth centuries, until it was over-come by the Mali empire, and then the Songhai, which extended its territory as far north as the city of Kano in the fifteenth century. Further to the east, around Lake Chad and further inland, the Kanem–Bornu empire extended its influence gradually from the eighth century until the sixteenth century, with efficient government, strong army, and wide commercial activities, until it succumbed to the Fulani Jihad, or Holy War, in the nineteenth century. In the southern forest zone the Ogo empire was strong enough to withstand the Fulani invasion of the 1830s; and there were city-states like that of Benin and Ife, whose culture is best known through magnificent bronze heads and other carvings, for ancient cities leave few traces unless built of stone in a dry climate.

The religious differences are at least as significant as the ethnic ones. The largest religion is Islam, with more than a third of the population as adherents. When the Sudanese kingdoms of the late Middle Ages were flourishing, Islam spread across the Sahara slowly, until the Fulani advanced in the Holy Wars of the nineteenth century and spread south through Hausaland as far as Ilorin. The ancient cities of the north – Kano, Sokoto, Katsina – are still almost entirely Moslem: there are numerous Koranic schools, new mosques are being built, and daily prayers, the Haj pilgrimage and the feast of Ramadan are firmly entrenched. The southern limit of the penetration of Islam was more or less along the natural boundaries of the Niger and Benue rivers.

Christianity made a tentative entry with the Portuguese in the sixteenth century, but was unable to make progress until after the British occupied Lagos in 1851, at first to use it for antislave trade operations, and subsequently extending their area of adminstration inland.[2] Christian missionaries followed in the wake of the administrators, and spread especially in the south, so that Christianity is now second in numbers after Islam. However, indigenous religions still have a strong influence in many rural communities. They usually have a belief in a Supreme Being and a world of spirits, with ancestor worship, magic and ritual, all affecting the crafts of weaving, carving, and singing, and integrated with community life.

The division between British and French territories in Africa was made by treaty in 1885; and seven years later the British brought to a close the long Yoruba wars, occupying Ibadan, Ogo and Benin. Early in this century the north was taken over by Lugard; and by 1914 the north and south were brought together as Nigeria, administered by indirect rule, which sought to ensure peaceful stability under the traditional rulers. When political groups began to emerge between the two World Wars, they were on regional lines, the three main parties being predominantly Hausa–Fulani in the north, Yoruba in the west, and Ibo in the east. After the end of the Second World War a series of constitutional conferences prepared the way for independence: in 1959 the North, West and East Regions became self-governing, and the Federation of Nigeria achieved independence in the following year. Fierce political rivalries nearly tore the new federation apart. In 1967, after oil was found in its area, and after massacres of Ibos and Hausas, the East attempted to secede, and three years of civil war followed before it was defeated. Since then reunification and development have gone apace, with the help of large oil revenues, under a military government which has divided the nation into twelve States in order to overcome the rivalry between the three former regions.

The rural Moslem north

Four out of five of Nigeria's population live in the countryside; and in the Moslem north, barely one in ten of the children attends school at present. Most of them live in communities made up of a small group of huts, or in small villages, their only links with the outside world being along rough tracks suitable for donkeys leading to their neighbouring small communities; in some cases within walking distance of a rough road along which a truck passes occasionally to collect produce or convey passengers to the nearest market. Their main preoccupation is with fetching water, gathering firewood

97

for cooking (even in very hot climates), and growing enough crops or tending goats or cattle to feed and provide money to clothe the families, with a visit to market keeping the weekly rhythm. It is way of life close to nature, with hardly any margin for survival if the seasonal rains fail, that has changed little through the centuries. In a state capital like Sokoto or Kano, the new civilisation of trucks, cars and men riding motorcycles with their flowing robes swept over one arm, still mixes with the old civilisation of cattle, sheep and goats, donkeys and camels; traditional houses of baked mud predominate in the city, and new concrete houses and offices are spread out on the periphery.

Slowly the new is invading the old in cities and towns, but the more remote rural communities are hardly touched as yet. Where the ground water is not too deep, pumps and tanks raised on stilts are being installed to provide a steady supply of good water, even for small communities; thus removing one chore from the daily tasks of children and women. If the supplies of natural gas in the delta area could be liquefied, bottled and distributed cheaply, as has been done in the Mediterranean, that would obviate the task of collecting firewood. In addition, new major and minor roads are being built; and in time, for it is a large country, the physical environment for rural living will be improved fundamentally. But it is also necessary for rural incomes to rise until they approach the level of wage earning or trading in cities, if a bare subsistence economy is to be changed to a modern cash economy. It follows that, if conditions of living and farming production are to be raised substantially there would have to be a coordinated development programme involving many aspects such as land tenure, family planning, crop improvement, animal husbandry, irrigation, marketing, cooperatives etc., and all with educational requirements which are being very imperfectly met at present.

Modernisation in the south

The early contacts with the Western world came through the coastal ports, and from them trade, administration, roads, mission schools, etc., spread inland, especially to the long established cities of the former kingdoms. More recently the finding of oil, and the greatly increased tempo of development, have given a tremendous stimulus to commercial activities – for which the Nigerians of the south, in particular the Yoruba, have a flair – and have also accelerated the growth of industries. Lagos and Ibadan have become two of the largest cities in Africa; Lagos is on a constricted site, and the combination of being federal capital, the main port, and also a state capital, has caused an extent of congestion which threatens breakdown. Moreover the congestion sharpens the tensions to be expected when miles of urban slums spread around the areas of prestige offices and comfortable homes. In spite of its humid climate, the general atmosphere is certainly not of lethargy or despair; for this is a nation determined to become modern at a gallop. A visitor to the South sees evidence of this on every side, with new housing, schools and colleges, offices and factories, roads, etc., rising like hesitant mushrooms. Planning and coordination are inadequate, docks and transport are hopelessly congested, yet the rate of economic growth is among the highest in the world. The pace of change is tremendous; and features characteristic of fast economic development are evident: (i) rapid inflation, which strikes hardest at the low paid workers; (ii) a shortage of all kinds of skilled workers, engineers, teachers, managers; (iii) high rate of unemployment of school leavers without skills; (iv) considerable migration from the countryside to live in towns and cities, some of which are long established, and which now house a fifth of the population (in towns over 20,000); (v) little improvement in agricultural production, which becomes less important in economic terms as industry develops under the direct and indirect stimulus of oil production, yet is crucial to rural development.

The first commercial discovery of oil was in 1956. Since then there have been three economic development plans. The first, for 1962–68, was disrupted by the civil war. The second, for 1970–74, was introduced in a hurry at the end of the war, and was largely ineffective. The third, for 1975–80, has taken advantage of experience, and is more promising. It gives more attention to agricultural growth, the improvement of communications, and to the extensive development of small and medium industry – with the aim of taking full advantage of the oil income while it lasts. The manpower implications have been assessed for the major needs of industry, commerce, administration, health etc., relating them to appropriate levels of training.[3]

The north–south contrast and educational development in Nigeria

In the south most children attend primary school, as many as 90 per cent in urban areas, and about 20 per cent go to secondary school. There are at present five universities in the south, at Ibadan, Nsukka, Lagos, Ife and Benin, and one in the north, namely Ahmadu Bello University at Zaria. In the Moslem north, where boys have been traditionally educated in Koranic schools and girls kept within the family, less than 10 per cent of the age group attend primary school, and under 1 per cent go to secondary school. The contrast between educational development in north and south creates a potential threat to cohesion of the federation. Moreover, it is a double contrast: between rural Moslem north, and urban south, predominantly Christian.

The feudalism of the Moslem north has retarded educational and economic development, but it has preserved a stable society, free of the tensions, unrest and violence which are features of most large cities. The respect of the young for the old, the cohesion of families, and the ordered hierarchy of the north contrast with the dynamic, fluid, economic competitiveness of the south; though here also local and kinship loyalties are powerful, with religion and folk cultures adding to the strong community feeling. The all pervading 'extended family' gives a form of innate socialism, supporting individuals, though also encouraging nepotism. However, the position of women is inferior to men, as always in Africa, and especially in Moslem societies. They have to work in the fields as well as rear children, provide meals, and do marketing; however, in this respect, as in others, the south is becoming westernised, especially in the small well educated sector, and the proportion of girls attending school is nearly as high as boys. Even these brief comments illustrate some of the conflicts between pressures for modernisation and the resistance of traditional societies and their leaders.

Now the federal government has decided that universal primary education shall be started in 1976, the primary schools being expanded to take in the whole group reaching six years of age in that year and each of the five succeeding ones to cover the full six years of primary schooling. It is a modest task for the south, and an impossible one for the north. However unrealistic it may be, it does express the overriding priority given to UPE by the government, and their belief that this is essential to incorporate the north into the modern Nigerian nation, and to preserve the unity of the federation.

While the main thrust will be to establish UPE in the minimum time, there will also be corresponding developments in other parts of the educational system: an increase in the number of secondary schools of various kinds, and of girls in them – at present the ratio of boys to girls is about 2 to 1 overall. Grammar schools will have technical courses, there will be more technical and commercial schools, and perhaps comprehensive schools in one state (these, like the experimental one of Aiyetoro, are comprehensive in the North American sense of having a full range of courses, not in the British sense of being nonselective neighbourhood schools). All secondary schools will continue to charge fees. Each state will have one or more government secondary schools, with good staffing and facilities, and there will also be federal government schools, admitting students from different states on a quota basis, in order to encourage national unity and to ensure that standards are not lowered by expansion. The wide variety of technical institutions, approaching a hundred, will be extended; and also the ten colleges of technology. Four more universities are proposed, which are likely to be at Jos, Calabar, Maiduguri, Sokoto or Kano. Altogether it is an ambitious plan, with the emphasis on expansion and not on innovation, though great efforts are being made to improve the primary school curricula and textbooks.

The school system follows the usual lines, in that promotion through the six years of the primary school depends on completing each year's work satisfactorily. Pressure on selection for secondary schools is kept down by fees. At the end of the fifth year, pupils take the West African School Certificate, and most get something, though only about a quarter do well enough to proceed to Sixth Form or the Basic Studies course at a university. The pyramid of the system is tall and narrow at the top; or, to be more precise, there is a broad based pyramid for the south, and one hardly more than a tenth of the breadth for the north, the latter having a very slender apex indeed. The aim of UPE is to expand the pyramid of the north to make it nearly equivalent to the south.

Even this brief account would be incomplete without a mention of Koranic schools. These are most numerous in Kano State, though there are also many in the adjacent north-eastern and north-western states. In Kano there are nearly twice as many children enrolled in Koranic, or Islamic, schools as in primary schools (it is estimated that the ratio was 50 to 1 in 1929, and 250 to 1 in 1914). The schools comprise more or less formal groups, with boys and girls sitting separately, varying in number up to about 30 or so, under a Malam, who does not have formal qualifications but is recognised as a teacher by the community. In Kano there is a strong desire to keep the Islamic schools separate, extending the subjects they teach, and qualifying for small grants; but in other states there is a movement to include Islamic studies within the curriculum of the primary school.

The political decision to bring in UPE very rapidly has required a crash programme to train more teachers, which means building and staffing training colleges, as well as building more schools. The strain on state Ministries of Education has been great, and inevitably shortages of resources cause delays. A serious difficulty is that the strain is greatest on the states which are weakest at ministry level, in the administrative skills of coordinated planning, in the inspectorate, supply of teachers, etc. In the event, expansion will probably be faster than if the federal government had not made its declaration on UPE, but not as fast as the plan indicates – which would certainly be beyond the scope of slowly changing attitudes in many northern communities.

E

Education in Nigeria: future problems

We have seen that Nigeria has planned a large expansion of its educational system, which has been inherited from the time when it was a British colony, and which is on similar lines to those of the advanced industrial countries; for that is what Nigeria aims to become in a relatively short time with the help of its oil revenues. Other countries with rapid industrial development in the last two or three decades, notably Japan and West Germany, have educational systems of a similar kind.

However, education has to contribute, as we have seen, not only to economic growth and meeting estimates of manpower requirements, but also to broader targets within the overall development plan, such as:

1 Rural development – and it is evident that the primary school in its present form is ill suited to this purpose.
2 Achieving a closer fit between the education in primary and secondary schools, and in colleges and universities, and employment opportunities; and this involves changing attitudes as well as providing training in skills – it involves far more than just manpower planning.
3 Education should form part of a coordinated programme to reduce the rate of population growth.

The first two of these have short term social and political implications. The third is no less important, but it is easier for a government to avoid the difficulties and problems involved without suffering in the short run.

The main emphasis is initially on expansion, as we have seen; it appears that, as it progresses, experience may well indicate that it should be modified in order to give a higher priority to the three social issues which have just been mentioned – for the evidence, although gathered from detailed studies in certain countries, seems to be of widespread application. Some of the implications will be reviewed in the concluding chapter.

Educational development: some political issues

The decision to make UPE the cornerstone of the broadly social, as distinct from economic, development of Nigeria was essentially a political one. The reasons for taking the decisions understandably override what might be described as professional considerations, for they are related – only four years after the end of the civil war – to the future stability of Nigeria as a nation.

There is a central problem in many nations enclosing a variety of cultural and economic conditions, and especially those with federal constitutions, concerning the extent to which education should express the cultural diversity, or aim at national unity. Thus, it could be argued that the Moslem north of Nigeria should have an appropriate form of education, Islamic and traditional; but this would tend to be divisive in a country where that is a risk to be avoided. Among the large nations, the USSR (which has more than twice the land area of China, USA or Canada – with Brazil next) provides an interesting example of federal diversity. It includes over a hundred distinct nationalities, newspapers are published in seventy-five languages, and each of the fifteen Union Republics has its own language – Russian is only the mother tongue of half the population, though it is the official language of the USSR. The Union Republics are divided into Autonomous Republics and Regions, and National Areas, to recognise the national minorities. Children are taught in their own language at school, and sometimes at university as well. Russian has to be learned, as the official language, and it is the policy to include a non-Soviet foreign language as well in all school curricula. The result of trying to provide for both local language and other cultural conditions, and also the national language and culture, places a heavy burden on the school curriculum.

The subcontinent of India shows how important the question of religion can be, for it was mainly religious differences between Hindus and Moslems that led to the division between the two nations of India and Pakistan at the time of independence in 1947, to the subsequent fighting between them, and the later tragic split between the two parts of Pakistan. Certainly the last of these divisions, separating Bangladesh from Pakistan, has produced nations which are hardly viable. Events since independence have been an endless struggle by the central government to preserve something of a unified balance in the face of a bewildering variety of ancient cultures, differences of race, language, social hierarchies, etc., and modernise this almost ungovernable mixture, with very limited natural resources and a population expanding faster than any hope of economic progress. Faced with almost overwhelming odds, the government has little help from education. Although four-fifths of the population is rural and depends on agriculture, Gandhi's ideas for village education have never been adopted, and there is now an inflated system of formal schooling, with a high rate of unemployment at the end. Fewer than half the children go to school, half of these drop out by class five, only one in five goes to secondary school and one in twenty-five to university, yet there is a serious overproduction of graduates. It is a system that not only fails to meet the evident needs, it even works against rural development and agricultural improvement. Education designed for a 'back to simple life in the countryside' movement has no chance of success, for that is what the young are struggling desperately through the school system to get away from, and they will go on struggling even when the odds are hopelessly against them. This cannot be changed easily, for India has striven to continue as a political democracy, sustaining much individual freedom to make choices, as far as these can be made within the confines of desperate poverty; and the hope of escape from this condition through education, however faint, is one of the choices many wish to preserve. Clearly the system of education cannot be changed by itself; and it seems as though it could only be fundamentally reformed as part of a reform of social organisation, land tenure, agricultural and industrial development, etc. Moreover, there can be little hope for the future unless the rate of population increase can be drastically cut, for it is growing from its present level of over 563 million (mid 1972) so fast that it will exceed 1000 million soon after the turn of the century, and disaster will come long before then, perhaps in the next few years.

Now that China has opened a discreet window on to the world at large, there is widespread concern to understand the revolution which has been enacted and is still going on. There is admiration because they carried through their revolution without foreign aid (after the initial Russian help), and became self sufficient for food; and they have almost succeeded in bringing their family size down to the level of a stable population, all of them remarkable achievements. Political conformity rules every personal activity, through the controlling committees which express the 'silent insistence of society'. One can hardly imagine this working in a society less habituated to conform as a result of deeply engrained custom, less willing to work hard and long for little reward, or less strong in self discipline. Even so, the 'cultural revolution' was deemed necessary to cleanse the body politic; and there may be further turbulence with changes of leadership. Nonetheless, the influence on the Third World of the political outlook and achievements of the new China are bound to be far-reaching; and they can be seen as forming a new culture out of the ancient traditional cultures, a culture in which the family persists though diminished in significance, and in which women are treated as the equal of men. In all respects education forms an integral part of the political and social framework of life, much of it being what we should describe as comprehensive indoctrination from early childhood and through-out life; for that is how it was conceived, as an essential driving force in the revolution.

Education has had the dual function of promoting change and preserving national unity in both Russia and China, despite the profound differences between the two countries. It had a similar function in the USA when immigrants were being absorbed in very large numbers, though with the emphasis on individual freedom and responsibility within an open democracy. Under these conditions the extent to which the culture of indigenous or immigrant minorities could be expressed in the educational system was limited, for the stress was on a common culture and on developing unifying attitudes and outlook.

Notes

¹ The income from oil, though massive, was only equivalent to $4 a head in 1970, compared to $37 for Iran and $125 for Venezuela. The figures would all be much higher now, though in more or less the same proportions. Nigeria's GNP per capita in 1972 was only $130 so that it is still a poor country.

² Although Britain passed an Act to abolish the slave trade in 1807, and the Emancipation Act in 1833, Acts to free slaves were not passed by France until 1848 and the United States until 1863, after the civil war. Slavery has continued in some Arab countries until recently.

³ The following references will give a general background to problems of development in Nigeria, in relation to education:

R. Hallet, *People and Progress in West Africa: An Introduction to the Problems of Development*, Pergamon, London, 1965.

B. O. Ukeji, *Education for Social Reconstruction*, Macmillan, Nigeria, 1966.

N. Otouti, *Western Education and Nigerian Cultural Background*, Oxford University Press, Ibadan, 1968.

D. Okafor-Omali, *A Nigerian Villager in Two Worlds*, Faber and Faber, London, 1965.

A. Peshkin, *Kanuri School Children: Education and Social Mobilization in Nigeria*, Holt, Rinehart and Winston, New York, 1972.

P. C. Lloyd, *Power and Independence: Urban Africans' Perception of Social Inequality*, Routledge and Kegan Paul, London, 1974.

E. Isichei, *The Ibo People and the Europeans: The Genesis of a Relationship – to 1906*, Faber, London, 1973.

P. J. Foster, *Education and Social Change in Ghana*, Routledge and Kegan Paul, London, 1965.

8   Educational Aims and Strategies for Development

Some general aims for education

Education involves both human aspirations and practical realities. It should provide for both. In developing countries it clearly does not meet either of them sufficiently, and there is a pressing need for reappraisal. There can obviously be no easy or straightforward way of providing for 'human aspirations and practical realities' when these are so different in kind, cover a wide field, and have complex relationships with economic, social, political and other aspects of development. It seems likely that the failure of education in developing countries during the last two or three decades to meet such aims as these has been the result of an oversimplified approach: education was regarded as synonymous with formal schooling, and expected to contribute to economic growth, and hopefully to improve social conditions. But education is not a separate affair, from which the good things flow naturally. It is now realised that education should form an integral part of overall development planning, in advanced industrial countries as well as in the Third World.[1]

The advanced countries have highly developed systems of education, with all young persons in full time schooling to between the ages of fifteen and eighteen, many going on to college or university, and widespread opportunities for part-time education, usually on vocational lines. In these countries there is pressure for more 'democratisation' of the educational system, more emphasis on 'learning' as opposed to 'teaching', and the development of an extensive and flexible range of opportunities to provide for 'recurrent education' throughout the life span. Increasingly in the advanced countries development is being thought of in terms of change, of maturing a system, rather than of continued expansion; and highly institutionalised systems of education, with large bureaucratic administrations, are slow in responding to changing circumstances.

The situation of Third World countries is different in that they do not yet have fully developed systems of formal schools, colleges, etc. In consequence they have an opportunity to incorporate modern ideas of non-formal education, using cheap technological aids, giving more attention to self-motivated learning as opposed to didactic instruction, seeking to reduce the constricting influence of regular examining, and thus developing a more flexible and responsive system of education. This would require a new outlook in their educational planning: a skilled creative approach, under vigorous political leadership, and some Third World countries are already showing their readiness to develop on these lines. If it can be achieved, they could find themselves having, within a decade or two, systems of education at least as modern as the advanced countries; perhaps more so, if large inflexible institutions form a smaller part of their overall provision.

With this possibility in mind, let us draw together some of the general aims for education in developing countries which have been discussed earlier in the book, and consider how they can serve as a basis in formulating strategies for development. There are too many variables between countries, as well as within them, and our understanding of their interaction is too imperfect, to enable us to begin to think in terms of 'models': the most we can hope for is some general principles which can serve as guidelines in the preparation of policies and programmes for educational development. We shall start by enumerating some of these aims or principles for planning, referring briefly to the earlier discussion of them:

1 *Overcoming abject poverty.* The first priority for some two-fifths of the population of developing countries, possibly as many as 800 million people, who are barely surviving in abject poverty on the margin of life, is to bring them up to a reasonable minimum standard of living (see chapter 5). Until this can be done, there is no sense in talking about giving them more scope for the expression of human qualities.

2 *Improving the 'quality of living'.* Once the physical standard of living is raised above a minimum, other qualities, including those set out in the Charter of Human Rights of the United Nations, become increasingly important. The notion of 'quality of living' refers to physical requisites, such as adequate food, shelter, clothing, health, etc.; conditions to allow individual development, such as education, freedom to enjoy democratic rights, etc.; and a rich social life in a community environment forming part of a just and reasonably egalitarian society (chapters 3 and 4). Inherent in this approach is the concept of self realisation of young people within the culture of their society.[2] These goals are similar for rich and poor countries, but the latter have more difficulty in providing the material needs. However, 'quality of living' is a relative term, and it can lead to satisfying conditions for living at very different economic levels. The problems of modern industrial cities show that material advancement does not necessarily produce a more satisfying environment for living.

3 *Rural development requires integrated planning*. In developing countries, which are predominantly rural, education contributes little to raising agricultural productivity or to improving qualities of living unless it is part of integrated plans or projects with these aims. This rarely happens, for education, agriculture, health, etc., usually come under separate ministries, with the result that aims are limited and coordination is weak (see chapter 5). The formal primary school fails to meet the needs by itself of rural development, and it should form part of a wider system.

4 *The development of the modern sector* requires a higher level of general education, and a whole range of technical, professional and administrative skills at intermediate and advanced levels. It creates a new élite, administrative as well as technological, with a large bureaucracy, widely separated from the mass of workers with low skills and the peasants in the countryside. The result is an extended society, with great disparity between the majority who are poor, and the élite minority who emulate the personal standards of living of the advanced countries. The processes of industrial and commercial growth tend to benefit the affluent minority; and spreading the advantages of economic progress more equitably raises political questions. Education has two functions amongst others: to meet the requirements for trained manpower at all levels, and it is also the system through which the new élite is largely selected (unless the selection is through wealth, nepotism etc.).

5 *Planning for a rural–urban society*. In most developing countries there is considerable movement of persons between urban and rural environments, although the net effect is usually a large scale migration from countryside to town or city, where it causes a rapid growth of urban slums. This migration is unlikely to diminish until rural development has been carried much further, and the disparity between urban and rural incomes has been greatly reduced (chapter 6). Clearly education has to meet different requirements in rural and urban settings, but it has also to be planned as a continuum. If education is related to different environments and cultures within a country, it has also to foster a sense of national unity (chapter 7).

6 *Problems of food supply and population growth* raise very serious issues on a national as well as a world level (chapter 2). Many developing countries, though predominantly rural, are unable to feed their fast growing populations. The present very rapid increase of population in many of them offsets their own efforts to develop; and it also threatens a world shortage of food before long, even if distribution between rich and poor nations were to become much more equitable – which will not happen easily as long as nationalism continues to be a dominant force, setting the sovereignty of each nation above the development of international cooperation.[3] At present most developing countries are giving higher priority to industrial than

rural development; and few are making concerted efforts to lower their rate of population increase as part of their development planning; and only integrated programmes seem to have a chance of success.

7 *Problems of unemployment* have become so serious as to deserve separate mention (chapter 6). While education cannot directly reduce unemployment, except by requiring more teachers, a reform of educational systems could do much to alleviate its impact, especially on young people leaving schools and colleges.

The functions of an educational system

The need for a reappraisal of the educational systems of developing countries has been stressed (chapter 1). In many of the poorer countries only half or fewer of the children go to school, and there is no prospect of these countries being able to expand their school systems much in the foreseeable future, especially when population is growing faster than resources. Moreover, the primary school, even with revised curricula, does not meet the kind of aims which have been sketched in outline in the preceding section: it is neither flexible enough, nor close enough to the requirements for development. In some countries, especially communist or strongly socialist ones, selection for secondary and more advanced education is made on a communal and political basis after a period of work. In others proposals have been made, and tried out on a small scale, to interpose a required period of work or national service between primary and secondary schools, or between secondary school and university. Many countries have some form of national service in teaching, rural welfare, development projects etc. as a requirement on completion of university or college studies; and these are intended to widen the outlook of the young persons, as well as contributing to national development. Another important line of development has emphasised the potential value of non-formal education, which can provide a flexible variety of local opportunities (chapter 5). For the most part these have been separate developments which have been initiated to meet certain problems, such as unemployment of the young, overproduction of secondary school pupils, reluctance of young graduates to work in isolated rural areas, etc. It is an appropriate time to consider whether such developments can be envisaged as components in a framework which is much broader than the usual system of education. With the aims or principles of the previous section in mind, it is possible to set out several main functions which should be covered:

1 To give all children a basic education sufficient to achieve literacy, to enable them as young people to read pamphlets, local news sheets, etc.;

to consider evidence; and to be able to decide what to do in practical situations in their lives.

2 To provide a continuing flow of information in practical learning situations, especially for youths and adults, covering better methods in agriculture, health, literacy and many aspects of community development, including family planning, as an integral part of overall development.

3 To provide 'modern learning systems' for those eager to carry their studies further in general education, in preparation for attending secondary schools or vocational institutes. If students in isolated rural communities were to take advantage of the learning packages without the help of specialist teachers, it would be essential for them to have sufficient attainment in basic education. Some tutorial help would generally be needed in rural centres or in urban areas.

4 To provide a range of secondary schools and vocational institutes, entry to the latter being at several levels: from primary via non-formal courses, or after junior or senior secondary school.

5 To provide a range of tertiary level institutions, including universities and specialised colleges.

6 All these aspects would be permeated by political ideology in communist countries, from the earliest preschool education up to, and including, university studies. In more democratic countries much less attention is usually given to political education, a situation inherited from the Western tradition. However, ways of encouraging a more democratic and less authoritarian atmosphere for learning should be considered, and also of giving recognition to the value of various forms of national service.

This is not intended to be a definitive statement of the functions of an educational system, which would in any case have to be thought out afresh in the light of the particular circumstances of each country. But it should give a sufficient basis to consider how these broad functions could be translated into a system of education.

The organisation of a comprehensive system of education

There are three fundamental questions to be resolved in planning a system of education, once its aims and functions have been decided, namely: what the components should be, how they should be related to each other, and how they should be administered.

It will be immediately apparent that the functions summarised in the previous section do not correspond with the structure of an orthodox system of education. This comprises a pyramid of three horizontal levels

111

first primary, then secondary, and tertiary at the top. In many developing countries the base is fairly broad, covering half or more of the age group, but the pyramid narrows rapidly towards its small apex. A child starting in the first grade of the primary school begins to ascend a ladder, going up one rung each year, until he or she is unable to continue for one reason or another and falls off – commonly with a sense of having failed to go as far up the ladder as he or she would have wished. The experience may be exhilarating for the few who reach the top, and their rewards are great; but for the many it is a disheartening process. Needless to say, the advanced countries have tried to make the system provide a common educational experience for all, with competitive selection which is required for some purposes in society postponed to a later age. This is not possible in the incomplete school provision of developing countries, which cannot take all children together through primary and secondary levels. An alternative approach, which could incorporate some of the forward looking ideas being discussed in industrial countries, has to be considered.

Let us now return to the first two questions at the beginning of this section, namely: what should the components be, and how should they be related to each other? The components will have to include both the formal institutions of schools, colleges, etc. and the arrangements for non-formal education. Their relationship should avoid being in strict sequence, like a ladder, with progress ruled by examinations. It would be foolish to think that examinations can be eliminated altogether, or replaced by something called 'objective' or 'aptitude' tests, but at least they should not dominate the whole system and the form of teaching in it as generally happens at present. The only way to relax the grip of formal instruction coupled with dominating examinations (which will certainly be difficult, even if supported by changes in wage differentials etc.) seems to be to incorporate non-formal education as a major component within the system. It would then serve functions 2 and 3 in the preceding section, leaving formal institutions to serve 1, 4 and 5.

The primary school would provide the foundation for all children, or as many as possible, the others having literacy classes and joining in the simpler non-formal activities. The scope of the primary school would not try to cover a full general education, for it would be supplemented by the subsequent non-formal provision. The latter would include organised courses – the 'modern learning systems' – and also a variety of less structured activities. Children who wished to proceed to secondary schools would take the organised courses, which would be entirely voluntary, so that motivation, ability and persistence would all play a part in deciding who would go on to secondary school. The age range for these non-formal activities could be wide. If it was thought desirable, a small quota could go direct from primary to secondary school, but only a minority so that the route through non-formal courses would be the normal one. Similarly, there could be an intercalation of a year or two between secondary school and university, if it seemed appropriate; and this could be in conjunction with some kind of national service.

A development on these lines would provide a network of opportunities, not related to examinations at specific ages; though there would be stated requirements from within the range of non-formal provision for admission to secondary schools. It is the overall system, and not the individual institutions, which would be 'comprehensive', a network of opportunities and not a ladder with most falling off.

Such a comprehensive system would necessitate an effective development of non-formal activities, including 'learning packages'. There would have to be a centralised production of resource material and courses, while leaving plenty of freedom for additional local initiatives. An appropriate form of administration would be essential. In some places, village teachers have been given the task of organising community development projects, and the reasons for success and failure can be analysed. Much seems to depend on local conditions, the way the teacher is paid for the dual responsibilities, and his relationship to the community on one hand, and to the local government and ministry on the other. Whatever pattern is followed, it would be essential to have a simple and effective administrative organisation. Equally important, a much greater share of educational finance would have to go to non-formal education than is usual at present.

A crucial feature of non-formal education is that it would not depend on trained teachers; and, being separate from the teachers' unions and the bureaucracy associated with schools, it would be far more flexible. Tutors for non-formal education would be persons in the community with appropiate skills, and the ability to maintain the interest of their students; and they would be paid on an appropriate hourly or part-time basis, unless they were associated with one of the many voluntary activities. The presecondary and prevocational courses would be more structured, and supported by 'learning packages', with the help of tutors when possible (chapter 5). These courses, like all non-formal education, would be entirely voluntary, but there would be built-in incentives because they would form the main route for admission to education at a secondary level, whether in formal secondary schools or vocational institutes. The range of non-formal activities would tend to be much wider in urban than rural areas; but in both they would depend on modern learning packages, incorporating the use of written material in conjunction with radio programmes, and also television when facilities were available.

The third question earlier in this section asked how the formal and non-formal components should be related to each other. They could be developed alongside one another as in many community schools, village colleges, etc., with the non-formal activites organised either by the head of the school or by a separate organising tutor. Alternatively the non-formal activities could be quite separate, as, for example, in Russia where the komsomols, which originated as political institutions and now give non-formal education, have separate buildings and staff in the cities, though they meet in schools in rural areas.

The development of a wide range of activities and structured courses within non-formal education would be the key to changing the present system of formal schooling to a more comprehensive educational system, offering more opportunities for young people as well as adults, and much less tied to examinations. When examinations cease to dominate the process of selection, and the motivation of children and young people has more chance of being expressed through the non-formal sector, then the authoritarian didactic instruction characteristic of primary and secondary schools in developing countries could begin to change. There will be strong resistance, but at least the whole situation will not oppose change, as it does now.

There is a widespread feeling that schools in developing countries are so deeply committed to authoritarian rote learning, which was commonly practised in the nineteenth century but is now believed to yield poor dividends, that children learn little. They do not learn to understand what they read, to express themselves freely and clearly, to think about ideas and practical questions; theirs is inert and passive response to instruction. The growth from this to modern active learning is a long and difficult process.[4] But it could make progress in a reformed comprehensive system, provided other influences were favourable – a more modern approach to the training of teachers, to inspection, and to curriculum development – all of these would have to be coordinated under strong leadership.

Strategies for development

Education is still in the centre of the political scene in developing countries. It has opened up the possibility for children of climbing into the privileged world of government service, and even if few children succeed in gaining this prize, and most are left behind as failures, yet the chance exists. No politician could lightly introduce a change which diminished this opportunity. Quotas, enforced periods of work between primary and secondary schools, and other restrictions are bound to rouse opposition; and they could only be more generally adopted as part of a wider reform which opens out new opportunities. That is why a reorganisation to provide a comprehensive system of education, incorporating non-formal as well as formal education, and replacing the single ladder of competitive schooling by a network of more open and varied opportunities, could prove to be acceptable. The strategy to be followed would depend on the political circumstances, and also on the existing educational system. For instance, in Nigeria as described in chapter 7, it would probably be desirable to have further development of formal primary schools in the north before moving towards a comprehensive system, because of the great disparity between north and south. But it would be desirable to make a start in the near future in developing a more comprehensive system, incorporating non-formal education, and with common components arranged in a flexible pattern, to cover all parts of the country. In Kenya, on the other hand, a rather different approach might be pursued; while Tanzania has already introduced reforms with some of these features. As we have seen, education is not a separate affair, but has to be planned as an integral part of development, and therefore closely related to the planning for agriculture, industry etc.; and indeed to meet all the aims set out early in this chapter.

Improving the quality of education raises professional as well as political issues.[4] It can only be done through a coordinated programme; and it may be necessary to use fresh approaches. For example, each teacher in an advanced country is to a large extent independent in his classroom, and it is rare for an experienced teacher to be responsible for how less experienced colleagues teach. The assumption is that every teacher is fully trained. This is not so in developing countries. It would be far more appropriate to have an organisation of senior and junior teachers, with the latter following the instructions of the former. The most exciting teaching I have seen in a developing country was when inspectors were supervising every week a group of poorly qualified teachers, working together with them as a team, with the support of new and detailed syllabuses and teachers' books. It is a technique that has been applied widely in agricultural extension work, using successful farmers as demonstrators and leaders in introducing new methods. In-service training courses for teachers are a useful stimulant, but produce little change unless associated with new curricula and teaching materials, and followed up persistently by inspectors, heads of schools, etc. Too often a teacher returning with new ideas from a training course is unable to overcome the resistance of the rest of the staff, and slides quickly back into former habits. Here again, a coordinated programme of curriculum development, and in-service training of all the staff of selected schools in the use of new books etc., is required; and this calls for skilled organisation and administration.

The need for applied research

Research and development is just as necessary to improve education, as to improve agriculture or health, but there are very few research institutes for education; because ministries of education are usually traditional in outlook. The emphasis should be on problems in the country – language teaching, the relationships between the educational system and employment, curriculum development, assessing the efficiency of different aspects of education in achieving their aims, finding out the problems which are holding back the educational progress of many children, etc. Without applied research on such problems, there is a very imperfect basis for educational planning, and little prospect of improving the quality of education. In most Third World countries there is at present little or no applied research in education, apart from the limited field of curriculum development; very much less than in medicine or agriculture, although expenditure on education is very high, often the largest item on the national budget. It is worth considering how different medicine would be today if there had been little research during the last few decades: for instance, if antibiotics and modern drugs had not been developed. Similarly in agriculture, if there had been none of the extensive genetical research leading to the 'green revolution' and modern methods of crop and animal husbandry. Broadly speaking, education has suffered from just this absence of research and development, and it is not surprising that it continues on the same labour intensive lines, with little support from even simple applications of modern technology, as it has done for many years. If the Third World countries are to develop modern comprehensive systems of education in place of the present inappropriate and out-of-date systems inherited from other countries, then the new policies which they decide on will have to be strongly supported by programmes of applied research and development – leaving long term research to the advanced countries which are better equipped for it. The developing countries are well able to seek advice when they want it, and make policy decisions about the kind of education they wish to develop. When it comes to implementing their policies, however, many developing countries will want help with new curricula and initiatives, especially in areas like the development of 'modern learning systems', new approaches to the organisation of community schools, modern methods for the initial and in-service training of teachers, and so on. Here – as with new drugs in medicine, or new breeds of agricultural plants or animals – advantage should be taken of research conducted in advanced countries, the application of which has to be worked out appropriately within each country. This would often involve action research in selected schools, carefully planned and assessed.

Policies and their implementation

A clear distinction has been made between the formulation of policies for the development of education, as part of overall development planning, and their implementation. It is an important distinction. The government of a country is responsible for formulating its policies in education, as in other spheres; and it should be left free to do so – unless it contravenes international standards of justice etc. – even when it wishes to seek assistance in implementing its policies.

We have seen that the educational policies inherited by many Third World countries are inappropriate as well as partial, making little or no provision for large numbers of children, especially in rural areas, and contributing insufficiently to economic or social development. In consequence we have considered how existing systems of education could be reformed to meet the functions required of them. There are a number of interesting and significant reforms being tried out in various countries, and the notion is propounded that all Third World countries should consider making further appropriate developments, which would depend on the situation in each country, in order to develop a comprehensive system of formal and non-formal education. This general aim has been more or less tacitly accepted by many countries when preparing their development plans for education.

There are, however, difficult problems over implementation. On some aspects the advanced countries have little experience to offer, especially since they have usually regarded education as a field for political and social discussion and not for research and controlled experiments. Indeed research in education has been singularly neglected by the advanced nations, and in consequence by UNESCO, in contrast to other UN agencies such as WHO, FAO or ILO. More research is needed, especially action research and the objective assessment of experimental developments; and also the free exchange of information about applied research. Unfortunately the province of education is large, varied and ill defined, in which it is at a disadvantage compared with WHO, FAO etc. For instance, the concept of 'recurrent education' has been favoured for some years by UNESCO, yet it is still only loosely defined, and few developments in this sphere have been critically assessed. Moreover, it makes little progress in the advanced nations which already have highly developed bureaucratic systems of formal education. It may well be that the Third World countries have a better opportunity to develop a more flexible and responsive system incorporating formal and non-formal education. The decision whether to do this, or to take the simpler course of developing more schools of the kind they have already, is theirs. But if they decided to plan more comprehensive systems on the lines outlined above, then they will need much assistance in implementing the new policies. It will be tragic if the assistance will not be forthcoming.

Notes

[1] E. Faure, *Learning to Be*, UNESCO, Harrap, London, 1972.
[2] R. D'Aeth, *Youth and the Changing Secondary School*, UNESCO Institute for Education, Hamburg, 1973.
[3] B. Ward and R. Dubos, *Only One Earth: The Care and Maintenance of a Small Planet*, Penguin, London, 1972.
[4] C. E. Beeby, *The Quality of Education in Developing Countries*, Harvard University Press, Cambridge, Mass., 1966.

Bibliography

In this short list attention is given mainly to books close to the theme of this book which have been published recently.

Agricultural Development Council, *The Contribution of General Education to Agricultural Development, primarily in Africa*, Agricultural Development Council, New York, 1965.

Ahamad, B. and Blaug, M. (eds), *The Practice of Manpower Forecasting: a Collection of Case Studies*, Elsevier, Amsterdam, 1973.

Anderson, C. A. and Bowman, M. J. (eds), *Education and Economic Development*, Aldine, Chicago, 1965.

Anderson, J., *The Struggle for the School*, Longmans, London, 1970.

Apthorpe, R. (ed.), *People Planning and Development Studies*, Frank Cass, London, 1970.

Bairoch, P., *Urban Unemployment in Developing Countries*, International Labour Organization, Geneva, 1973.

Barratt, J. and Louw, M. (eds), *International Aspects of Over-Population*, Macmillan, London, 1972.

Batten, T. R., *Communities and Their Development*, Oxford University Press, London, 1957.

Beckford, G. L., *Persistent Poverty: Underdevelopment in Plantation Economies of the Third World*, Oxford University Press, New York, 1972.

Beeby, C. E., *The Quality of Education in Developing Countries*, Harvard University Press, Cambridge, Mass., 1966.

Benjamin, B., Cox, P. R. and Peel, J. (eds), *Population and the New Biology*, Academic Press, London, 1974.

Bereday, G. Z. F., *Essays on World Education: the Crisis of Supply and Demand*, Oxford University Press, New York, 1969.

Berry, B. J. L., *The Human Consequences of Urbanization*, Macmillan, London, 1974.

Blaikie, P. M., *Family Planning In India: Diffusion and Policy*, Arnold, London, 1975.

Blaug, M., Layard, R., and Woodhall, M. *The Causes of Graduate Unemployment in India*, Allen Lane, London, 1969.

Blaug, M. *Education and the Employment Problem in Developing Countries*, International Labour Organization, Geneva, 1973.

Brokensha, D., and Hodge, P., *Community Development: an Interpretation*, Chandler Publishing, San Francisco, 1969.

Brown, L. R., *In the Human Interest: a Strategy to Stabilize World Population*, W. W. Norton, New York, 1974.

Bunting, A. H., (ed.), *Change in Agriculture*, Praeger, New York, 1970.

Callaway, A., *Educational Planning and Unemployed Youth in Africa*, Commonwealth Secretariat, London, 1973.

Cameron, J. and Dodd, W. A., *Society, Schools and Progress in Tanzania*, Pergamon, Oxford, 1970.

Castle, E. B., *Education for Self-Help*, Oxford University Press, London, 1972.

Connell, J., *The Evolution of Tanzanian Rural Development*, Institute of Development Studies, Sussex University, Brighton, Communication Series 110, 1973.

Centre for the Study of Education in Changing Societies, *Educational Problems in Developing Countries*, Walters-Noordhoff, Groningen, 1969.

Coombs, P. H., *The World Educational Crisis – a Systems Analysis*, Oxford University Press, New York, 1968.

Coombs, P. H., Prosser, R. C., and Ahmed, M., *New Paths to Learning for Rural Children and Youth*, International Council for Educational Development, Essex, Connecticut, 1973.

Coombs, P. H. and Ahmed, M., *Attacking Rural Poverty: How Non-Formal Education Can Help*, Johns Hopkins University Press, Baltimore, 1974.

Curle, A., *Educational Problems of Developing Societies: with Case Studies of Ghana and Pakistan*, Praeger, New York, 1969.

Curle, A. *Educational Strategy for Developing Societies*, Tavistock, London, 1963/2nd ed. 1970.

Curle, A., *Education for Liberation*, Tavistock, London, 1973.

D'Aeth, R., *Youth and the Changing Secondary School*, UNESCO Institute for Education, Hamburg, 1973.

Dejene, T. and Smith, S. E., *Experiences in Rural Development* (bibliography for Africa), American Council on Education, Washington, 1973.

Dieuzeide, H., *Educational Technology and the Development of Education*, UNESCO, IEY, Paris, No. 8, 1970.

Drake, M. et al., *The Population Explosion: an Interdisciplinary Approach*, Open University Press, Bletchley, 1971.

Dumont, R., *False Start in Africa* (Translated from: *L'Afrique noir est mal partie*), Deutsch, London 1966/2nd ed. 1969.

Dwyer, D. J. (ed.), *The City in the Third World*, Macmillan, London, 1974.

Fagen, R. R., *The Transformation of Political Culture in Cuba*, Stanford University Press, Stanford, 1969.

Faure, E., *Learning to Be*, UNESCO Harrap, Paris/London, 1972.

Federal Ministry of Education, Nigeria, *Investment in Education* (Report of Ashby Commission), Federal Ministry of Education, Lagos, 1960.

Fitzpatrick, J. P. (ed.), *Educational Planning and Socio-Economic Development in Latin America*. Centro Intercultural de Documentacion, Cuernavaca, Mexico, 1966.

Foster, P. J., *Education and Social Change in Ghana*, Routledge and Kegan Paul, London, 1965.

Foster, P. J. and Zollberg, A. R. (eds), *Ghana and the Ivory Coast: Perspectives in Modernization*, Chicago University Press, Chicago, 1971.

Foster, P. J. and Sheffield, J. R. (eds), *Education and Rural Development*, The World Year-Book of Education, 1974, Evans, London, 1974.

Gaitskell, A., *Gezira: a Story of Development in the Sudan*, Faber and Faber, London, 1959.

Galbraith, J. K., *The Underdeveloped Country*, Canadian Broadcasting Council, Toronto, 1965.

Gale, L., *Education and Development in Latin America*, Routledge and Kegan Paul, London, 1969.

Goulet, D., *The Cruel Choice*, Atheneum, New York, 1971.

Graham, C. K., *The History of Education in Ghana*, Cass, London, 1972.

Griffin, K., *The Political Economy of Agrarian Change – an Essay on the Green Revolution*, Macmillan, London, 1974.

Griffiths, V. L., *The Problems of Rural Education*, International Institute for Educational Planning, Paris, 1968.

Hallet, R., *People and Progress in West Africa: an Introduction to the Problems of Development*, Pergamon, Oxford, 1965.

Hanson, J. W., and Brembeck, C. S. (eds), *Education and the Development of Nations*, Holt, Rinehart and Winston, New York, 1966.

Hatch, J., *Tanzania: a Profile*, Praeger, New York, 1972.

Hawes, H. W. R., *Planning the Primary School Curriculum in Developing Countries*, International Institute for Educational Planning, Paris, 1972.

Hunter, G., *Best of Both Worlds? A Challenge on Development Policies in Africa*, Oxford University Press, London, 1967.

Hunter, G., *The Administration of Agricultural Development – Lessons from India*, Oxford University Press, London, 1970.

International Labour Organization, *Towards Full Employment: a Programme for Colombia*, ILO, Geneva, 1970.

International Labour Organization, *Matching Employment Opportunities and Expectations: a Programme of Action for Ceylon*, ILO, Geneva, 1971.

International Labour Organization, *ILO: Scope, Approach and Content of Research-Oriented Activities of the World Employment Programme*, ILO, Geneva, 1972.

International Labour Organization, *Employment, Incomes and Equality: a Strategy for Increasing Productive Employment in Kenya*. ILO, Geneva, 1972.

International Labour Organization, *Employment and Incomes Policy for Iran*, ILO, Geneva, 1973.

Isichei, E., *The Ibo People and the Europeans: the Genesis of a Relationship – to 1906*, Faber, London, 1973.

Jephcott, P., *Homes in High Flats*, Oliver and Boyd, London, 1972.

Johnson, S., *The Population Problem*, David and Charles, Newton Abbot, 1973.

Jolly, R. (ed.), *Education in Africa: Research and Action*, East Africa Publishing House, Nairobi, 1969.

Jolly, R., Seers, D. and Singer, H., 'The Pilot Missions Under the World Employment Programme,' included in *Strategies for Employment Promotion*, ILO, Geneva, 1973.

Kabwasa, A. and Kaunda, M. M. (eds), *Correspondence Education in Africa*, Routledge and Kegan Paul, London, 1973.

King, J., *The Planning of Non-Formal Education in Tanzania*, International Institute for Educational Planning, Paris, 1967.

Langley, J. A., *Pan-Africanism and Nationalism in West Africa 1900–1945*. Oxford University Press, London, 1973.

Lee, H. P., 'Education and Rural Development in China Today', in *World Year-Book of Education*, 1974, pp. 209–233, Evans, London, 1974.

Llewellyn-Jones, D., *Human Reproduction and Society*, Faber and Faber, London, 1974.

Lewis, L. J., *Society, Schools and Progress in Nigeria*, Pergamon, Oxford, 1965.

Little, K., *West African Urbanization: a Study of Voluntary Associations in Social Change*, Cambridge University Press, London, 1965.

Lloyd, P. C. *Power and Independence: Urban Africans' Perception of Social Inequality*, Routledge and Kegan Paul, London, 1974.

McMeekin, R. W., Jr., *Educational Planning and Expenditure Decisions in Developing Countries, with a Malaysian Case Study*, Praeger, New York, 1975.

McNamara, R. S., 'Address to Board of Governors', World Bank, Washington, September 30, 1974.

Mahgoub, M. A., *Democracy on Trial*, Deutsch, London, 1974.

Malassis, T., *Développement Economique et Programmation de l'Education Rurale*, UNESCO, Paris, 1966.

Malthus, T. R., *An Essay on the Principle of Population*, 1789, Reprinted by Macmillan, London, 1965.

Markovitz, I. L., *Leopold Sedar Senghor and the Politics of Négritude*, Atheneum, New York, 1969.

Massé, P., *La Crise du Développement*, Editions Gallimard, Paris, 1973.

Mead, M., *New Lives for Old: Cultural Transformation – Manus 1928–1953*. Morrow, New York, 1953 (and later eds).

Mende, T., *From Aid to Re-Colonization*, Harrap, London, 1974.

Mesa-Lago, C. (ed.), *Revolutionary Change in Cuba*, Pittsburgh University Press, Pittsburgh, 1971.

Moraes, D., *A Matter of People*, Praeger, New York, 1974.

Moumoni, A., *L'Education en Afrique*, Maspero, Paris, 1964.

Mphahlele, E., *The African Image*, Faber, London, 1974.

Najman, D., *Education in Africa: What Next?*, Editions 2000, Paris, 1972.

Nduka, O., 'Towards a National Policy on Education in Nigeria', *Prospects*, UNESCO 3, 3, 438–50, 1973.

Nekby, B. *CADU: an Ethiopian Experiment in Developing Peasant Farming*, Prisma, Stockholm, 1971.

Nyerere, J. K., *The Arusha Declaration*, Government Printer, Dar es Salaam, 1967.

Nyerere, J. K., *Education for Self-Reliance*, Government Printer, Dar es Salaam, 1967.

Nyerere, J. K., *Socialism and Rural Development*, Government Printer, Dar es Salaam, 1968.

Ogunsanwo, A., *China's Policy in Africa 1958–1971*, Cambridge University Press, London, 1974.

Okafor-Omali, D., *A Nigerian Villager in Two Worlds*, Faber and Faber, London, 1965.

O'Kelly, E., *Aid and Self-Help: a General Guide to Overseas Aid*, Knight, London, 1973.

Ominde, S. H. and Ejiogu, C. N. (eds), *Population Growth and Economic Development in Africa*, Heinemann, London, 1972.

Organization for Economic Cooperation and Development, *Educational Policies for the 1970's: General Report of the Conference on Policies for Educational Growth*, OECD, Paris, 1970.

Otouti, N., *Western Education and Nigerian Cultural Background*, Oxford University Press, Ibadan, 1968.

Peshkin, A., *Kanuri School Children: Educational and Social Mobilization in Nigeria*, Holt, Rinehart and Winston, New York, 1972.

Raper, A. F., *Rural Development in Action – the Comprehensive Experiment at Comilla, East Pakistan*, Cornell University Press, Ithaca, 1970.

Resnick, I. N. (ed.), *Tanzania: Revolution by Education*, Longmans, Arusha (Tanzania), 1968.

Schumacher, E. F., *Small is Beautiful*, Blond and Briggs, London, 1973.

Sheffield, J. R., and Diejomaoh, V. P., *Non-Formal Education in African Development*, African American Institute, New York, 1972.

Sheffield, J. R., *Education in Kenya: an Historical Study*, Teachers College Press, New York, 1973.

Singer, H. and Jolly, R., 'Unemployment in an African Setting: Lessons of the Employment Strategy Mission to Kenya', International Labour Review, Geneva, 107, 2, Feb., 1973.

Smith, T. E., (ed.), *The Politics of Family Planning in the Third World*, George Allen and Unwin, London, 1973.

Stamp, E., *The Hungry World*, Arnold, Leeds, 1967/2nd edition, 1972.

Streeten, P. *The Frontiers of Development Studies*, Macmillan, London, 1972.

Symonds, R. and Carder, M. *The United Nations and the Population Question*, Chatto and Windus, London, 1973.

Turnham, D., *The Employment Problem in Less Developed Countries: a Review of Evidence*, OECD Development Centre, Paris, 1971.

Ukeji, B. O., *Education for Social Reconstruction*, Macmillan, Lagos, 1966.

Vaizey, J., et al., *The Political Economy of Education*, Duckworth, London, 1972.

Van Rensburg, P., *Report from Swaneng Hill – Education and Employment in an African Country*, Dag Hammarskjold Foundation, Uppsala, 1974.

Wall, D., *The Charity of Nations: the Political Economy of Foreign Aid*, Macmillan, London, 1973.

Ward, B. and Dubos, R., *Only One Earth: the Care and Maintenance of a Small Planet*, Penguin, London, 1972.

World Bank and Institute of Development Studies, *Redistribution with Growth*, Oxford University Press, London, 1974.

World Bank, *Rural Development: Sector Policy Paper*, World Bank, Washington, 1975.

World Bank, *Education Sector Policy Paper*, World Bank, Washington, 1974.

Worsley, P., *The Third World*, Weidenfeld and Nicolson, London, 1969.

Index

The Author

Professor Richard D'Aeth was educated at Cambridge and Harvard Universities. He gained experience in research and teaching and as one of HM Inspectors of schools; then became the first Professor of Education in the newly established University of the West Indies. He is now Director of the School of Education at Exeter University, where he continues his interest in teacher education and educational problems in the Third World.